1368 DAYS

An American POW in WWII Japan

a memoir by

PETER B. MARSHALL

Edited by Cynthia Marshall Hopkins

LUMINARE PRESS

WWW.LUMINAREPRESS.COM

1368 Days: Memoirs of a WWII Japanese POW
©2017 Peter B. Marshall

Printed in the United States of America

Cover Design: Claire Flint Last

Luminare Press
438 Charnelton, Suite 101
Eugene, OR 97401
www.luminarepress.com

ISBN: 978-1-944733-16-2
LCCN: 2017932956

For Faye

Table of Contents

COMING HOME

Prologue

THERE ARE NOT MANY OF US WWII POWS LEFT NOW. I'M 96 years old and have outlived everyone I knew who was captured by the Japanese on Guam the day after the Pearl Harbor attack. Mosher, my best buddy in prison camp, and I had vowed to keep each other alive during our captivity. Mo died last summer. His caretaker told me that in his last days he continued to say that he had to stay alive to "keep Pete alive." When I wonder aloud to my family why I have survived for so long, they tell me it is so I can tell my story.

Our experiences should be remembered, so I've written down what happened during the 1368 days we were prisoners. This is my story, of course, but all of us in Zentsuji and Osaka POW camps went through those 1368 days together. Not all of us made it home. The war was a defining time in all of our lives, with many delayed physical and mental consequences. The tuberculosis I contracted in the camps wasn't diagnosed for over a year after the war's end, just as I was about to become a father.

I didn't talk about my experiences for many decades. I shed no tears. I was thankful to have survived and have a life with a wife and daughters. Still, the painful memories were always deep down inside. They finally surfaced in 1995 with the many public observances of the fiftieth anniversary of the end of WWII. Soon afterwards, I went into the VA hospital for a checkup, and a young intern who saw the POW stamp on my medical file asked me how long I had been a prisoner. That was all it took. The tears began to flow and I couldn't stop them.

The doctor made me agree to a session with the hospital psychiatrist. I ended up having two one-hour sessions within a couple of weeks, and probably went through a box of Kleenex at each. I thought at the time that I had finally gotten it out of my system. I thought I was okay, but the doctor strongly advised me to tell my story to my family and to continue sharing my story with others. I wrote down what I remembered of those 1368 days soon afterward. A few years later I sent my story to the Lebanon Daily Record, the newspaper of the town near where I grew up in Missouri. I didn't realize it at the time, but their publication of my story set in motion events that eventually made a huge difference for the better in my life.

In the past decade I have been honored in my home town of Prescott Valley, Arizona. There have been interviews and articles in the local newspapers. I have spoken at POW/MIA ceremonies held by the local VA hospital for high school students in the area. I was videotaped for the Library of Congress archives. All of this personal history sharing has helped me, and I feel good that future generations will learn what happened. I believe strongly that our youth need to understand about war and its consequences.

I had six brothers, five of whom served active duty in WWII along with me. An older brother Felix, now 100 years old, survived the bombing of Pearl Harbor. My parents must have worried constantly about the safety of their sons. All of us returned home alive.

I come from a large family whose many children and grandchildren have asked me to share my experiences. My daughters strongly urged me to put my life story together in this book. My wife, Faye, originally typed it all for me. My daughters recently retyped everything to save it electronically. They encouraged me to add some stories about growing up on Walnut Glen Farm during the Depression, the tenth of twelve children. I believe my upbringing played a big role in helping me survive captivity and endure the aftermath when I returned home, so I begin my story there.

I sincerely hope my story may help future generations.

WALNUT GLEN

Twelve Children

I WAS BORN FEBRUARY 21, 1921 AT 11:00 A.M. ON WALNUT GLEN farm in Long Lane, Missouri. I was named after my father, Peter Breckenridge Marshall; however, on the birth certificate the doctor put my name as Peter B. Marshall. Until I graduated from high school and left home, I was known as Peter B.

Papa married a cousin from Mississippi, Nora Haddick, in 1900. His mother and Mama's step-grandmother were sisters, so they were cousins by marriage, not blood kin. Papa was thirty-one and Mama sixteen when they married. By all accounts, theirs was a happy, loving union from the start.

They lived on Papa's eighty acre farm, eventually purchasing an additional forty acres. Mama named the farm Walnut Glen. There they raised twelve children—seven boys and five girls—born between 1901 and 1927. I was the tenth child, the fifth son.

My family lived through the period of World War I—for which Papa was too old and his sons too young to fight—the passage of women's suffrage and the Great Depression. We had no car, no central heating, and no indoor bathroom. Our farm was miles from the nearest school or town.

Our large family made it through these difficult years in a number of ways. Besides farming, Papa had a number of enterprises that he ran at various times from the farm. He ran a small home tomato canning factory. He had a broom-making machine and a fence-making machine and a mill.

During the Depression he hired himself out with his saw rig. We had produce from our garden to eat. We had a few cows and chickens that brought in a little bit of money. We hunted and fished.

My sister Mabel was the firstborn. She was twenty years older than me, already married, a wife and mother when I was born. Her husband Otto was a WWI veteran. They had eight children and lived near Walnut Glen. I lived with their family for nearly a year during 1934-35 when Otto worked in the Civilian Conservation Corps camps for WWI vets. There has always been a special bond between me and her children, who are more like brothers and sisters to me than nieces and nephews.

My oldest brother, Jerome, was surrounded by sisters growing up, but he was fortunate to have known Papa as a young man. I didn't know Jerome when I was a boy for he lived in Ashland, Kansas. We only saw one another during family visits. He was too old for the draft in WWII.

Third oldest was Corrine, whom I also did not know as she and her husband moved to Oregon when I was very young.

I have some early memories of my sister Edith, although she was also an adult by then. She played a role in introducing me to my future wife. She and her husband eventually moved to Tucson, Arizona, just a few hours away from me and my own family.

I knew Ethel the best of my four oldest sisters. When she left home to work, she would send Mama some money to buy us little kids shoes for school. She sent me money to buy my high school class ring. She helped pay off the mortgage on Walnut Glen in 1930. She married and moved to a ranch in Kit Carson, Colorado and had three children.

My brother Mack was ten years older than me and I have many fond memories of him growing up. At an early age he took on many of Papa's responsibilities for running the farm. Mack was drafted in 1944 and saw a lot of action in France and Germany. He and his family remained in the nearby town of Lebanon, where he was well known and liked.

My sister Harriet was a bit of a tomboy. Mama had a lot of children when I came along and, I've been told, gave responsibility for tending me to Harriet. She married twice. Her second husband died young and left her to raise their four children alone. She wound up close to our sister Corrine outside of Canby, Oregon. Her children still live on the family acreage there.

Felix, five years older than me, is my only surviving sibling as of this writing. He took responsibility at an early age for running the family household, helping with cooking and getting the younger children off to school. He joined the marines from 1935–39 and served in China. In 1939 he joined the navy. He was on the USS Tern in Pearl Harbor when the Japanese bombed on December 7, 1941. He survived. He lives just outside of Lebanon, Missouri with his wife of seventy-two years.

Donald was two years older than me. He tried farming right out of grade school, but was drafted in 1940 and became an army cook. After the war, he and his wife moved to Ventura, California where they raised three sons.

Billy was two years younger than me and I knew him the best of all my siblings. He joined the marines shortly after Pearl Harbor. After the war was over, he tried his hand at farming Walnut Glen, but he was not able to make a living at it. He moved his family to Phoenix, where he ran a gas station. He had three daughters. His family lived just a few

Ten of the twelve Marshall children. Peter is the baby on his mother's lap. Felix is between his parents.

minutes down the road from mine in Phoenix and we became very close. He was one of my best friends. When he died of a sudden heart attack in 1972 I was devastated.

Stanley was the youngest. He was only twelve when I left to join the Navy, so we didn't get to know each other well. When the war was over he earned a BS in electronics and then a PhD. He taught at Missouri University, Rolla, where his widow still lives.

Only Felix, age 100, and I, age 96, are left of the twelve children of Peter and Nora Marshall of Walnut Glen.

Latimer School

IN 1905 MY FATHER BUILT THE NEW LATIMER SCHOOL BUILD-ing that served the area's elementary needs until 1952. Papa furnished the lumber and built the one-room building for $350. When I started school in 1926, the grades of primer (like kindergarten) through the eighth were taught. The first four grades were taught every year. The fifth and seventh grades were taught one year and the sixth and eighth grades were taught the next year. If you began school the wrong year, you either spent two years in the fourth grade or skipped the fifth grade (if you were a good enough student). Upon completion of the eighth grade, we were given a written examination issued by the Dallas County superintendent of schools. I had no problem with the exam. All in all, I was a good student.

With the exception of the eighth grade teacher, Burnist Henson, each day began with about fifteen minutes singing or Bible study, depending on the teacher. Mr. Henson brought the day's precious newspaper to class and reviewed the world news. I think every student really enjoyed this. After the first fifteen minutes were up, the teacher hit a desk bell. First graders then took their seats on a bench facing the teacher. When the class period was over the teacher would again hit the bell and the first graders returned to their seats. The same routine would be used for each grade's class. There were fifteen minute recesses mid-morning and mid-afternoon and an hour for lunch.

On most Fridays there were special programs after the last recess. This was often a ciphering contest. The teacher appointed two of the top students as team captains. They wrote their names at the top of the black board. They then took turns selecting members of their teams until all the students, about twenty-five or so, had been selected. The last name on each list would compete against each other. The loser's name would be crossed out and the next on the list would be the new challenger. This person could name whether the problem to be solved involved addition, subtraction, etc. Sometimes, instead of ciphering, we had geography contests or spelling bees.

Three times during the school year we held special programs for the public. The first, a fund raiser held in the fall, was a pie supper (sometimes called a box supper). The women, married and unmarried alike, each baked a pie and brought it to the school in a fancy wrapped box to be auctioned off. The first event of the evening was a play put on by the students. Then the boxes were auctioned off, each to the highest bidder. This was followed by contests as to who was the biggest tobacco chewer, which couple was most likely to get married, who was the most hen-pecked husband or the best looking girl, etc. Each nominee received ten votes for each dime donated. All the proceeds went to the school. The winners received prizes.

In winter we had a special Christmas play. Students drew names for the exchange of gifts. However, the biggest program of the year was the one held on the last day of school. The doors were taken off their hinges and placed on the trestles to form a huge table and we had a pot luck dinner. The adults took part in activities, including ciphering contests and singing. One of my favorite songs sung in school was "Hurrah,

hurrah, we'll put our books away..." sung to the tune of *Marching through Georgia*. In 1956 I was at the Center for Disease Control in Atlanta, Georgia for three weeks of special training in serological techniques. It was a tough three weeks, and on the last Friday afternoon after getting off the bus and beginning the walk to my hotel, relieved that the training was over, I found myself humming my old school song. After getting dirty looks from the people I passed, I suddenly realized I was in Georgia, and stopped humming.

Except for the eighth grade year we had no organized games. One year one game was popular; the next year some other game took its place. My favorite games were shinny, rounders, one-eyed cat and stilts. Shinny was a form of ground hockey using an empty tin can as a puck. I still have scars on my shins from those games. Rounders and one-eyed cats were forms of baseball. We played basketball and volleyball whenever we had a ball that was pumped up, which wasn't very often.

Stilts was a game of my own invention. I got the idea from reading about the Knights of the Round Table. You drew a circle about eight to ten feet in diameter. Two people would duel each other on stilts within the circle. The first to get knocked out of the circle or off his stilts was the loser. I introduced this game when in the seventh grade. It didn't take.

Just across the road in front of Latimer school were a bunch of young white oak and post oak trees. I read Tarzan in the comics in the newspapers and wanted to be just like him. During recesses and the lunch hour, my cousin Carl D. Marshall and I played Tarzan, going from tree top to tree top. The young trees bent under our weight enough for us to grab a limb of the tree next to it. Our game came to an end when Carl fell from pretty high up and cut his head open on a rock. The other kids swore they could see part of his brain. The adults took him to the doctor who stitched him up. By the time I saw him again, he was already bandaged. He didn't seem to have any lingering after effects, but the teacher wouldn't let us play Tarzan any more.

Sometime during the early 1930s, Papa purchased a couple of donkeys for us kids to ride to school. We used them off and on for a few years, but overall I didn't think it was a great idea. I enjoyed the fellowship of the other students walking to and from school. I'll give you an example from seventh grade. My brothers Billy and Stanley and I left the house about 8:00 a.m. After walking nearly one-half mile, we were joined by four of the Dills children. We seven then took a short cut (except in muddy weather), and at about the half-way point (one and one-half miles from our home) we reached the creek between the Ed Wilkerson and Jasper Wilkerson places. Here we usually were joined by two Jackson girls, two Wilkerson boys and one Wilkerson girl. On a quiet morning you could hear the 8:30 school bell ring. There were about twelve of us that arrived at the school together about 9:00 a.m. The road home usually took us about thirty minutes longer. During the first quarter mile our group included the Hash brother and sister and the two Downing boys. On the way home we were all always hungry. Jasper Wilkerson always left the apples on a couple of trees for us to snack on.

Chores

THE FIRST CHORE I REMEMBER WAS KEEPING THE WOOD BOX for the cook stove filled. My brother Billy and I shared most chores. We weren't very old when we began sawing backlogs for the fireplace. I enjoyed getting the winter wood supply in. The worst jobs we had were thinning cane, stripping cane and cutting sprouts.

When Papa purchased an additional forty acres during the early 1920s, it was mostly trees. He had about half the trees cut down and turned into pasture land, but every spring the sprouts from the cut down trees would come back up. Billy

Clockwise from upper right:
Mack, Peter, Stanley, Billy, Donald, Felix.

and I cut thousands of sprouts during our elementary school years. Despite doing so during the proper phase of the moon, those sprouts kept coming back.

I think I began milking at about age ten. I enjoyed separating the milk. At first we sold sweet cream which was picked up daily by the cream man, who was paid by the dairy he took his supply to. Once a week he delivered a check to each customer. For a while, this was our only source of regular income, although eventually we also sold sour cream, which was picked up about twice a week.

Uncle Joe Marshall Dies

THIS WAS A VERY TRAUMATIC EXPERIENCE FOR ME. UNCLE Joe, Papa's older brother by four years, lived on a farm bordering ours. He had been confined to a wheel chair for over a year before he died. I used to visit him and listen to his wild stories. His funeral at Harmony Church cemetery was the first funeral I ever attended. I was ten years old. That night I realized that someday I would have to die. I was terrified.

After Uncle Joe's death, Mama decided that his widow, Aunt Lovey, shouldn't be alone at night and one of us kids should sleep over there. Aunt Lovey's children were all away from home at that point. Billy and I started out taking turns, but soon it became my responsibility alone. This went on for about two years, but if Mama had only known what went on at Aunt Lovey's, she wouldn't have let us stay there but one night.

Aunt Lovey's cat had been killing her little chicks and she asked me to kill the cat. She loaded up the 12-gauge shotgun. I had never fired a shotgun before, but I did as Aunt Lovey told me. While the cat was drinking milk from a stonemason container about twenty feet away, I aimed and pulled the trigger, destroying both cat and container. The kick of the gun knocked me over backwards. Aunt Lovey really bawled me out for destroying her stonemason container.

On another occasion, we found a large black snake in the house. I grabbed some blacksmith tongs and got hold of the snake. Aunt Lovey loaded a .32 caliber pistol for me. Then, with one hand holding the snake, I blew its head off. Unfortunately, I also blew a hole in the floor.

One night Aunt Lovey woke me up because there was a noise in the chicken house. By this time, I was getting used to the guns. I loaded and cocked the .32. Aunt Lovey held a large flashlight. We headed out in the dark to the chicken house. An opossum had gotten a hen and was eating it. I killed the opossum with one shot. Usually I left for Aunt Lovey's after dinner with my family, but the night after killing the opossum, I told Mom that Aunt Lovey was fixing me dinner. We had baked opossum with some potatoes. I liked it.

Feeding a Large Family

IT SEEMED WE HAD HOT CEREAL WITH SUGAR AND MILK MOST mornings. When we had cornmeal mush or rice, Mom always cooked about twice what we would eat for breakfast and fried up the leftover corn meal mush for dinner (the noon meal, what we now call lunch). Leftover rice was made into a pudding. Graham mush was cooked in the proper amounts as there wasn't much you could do with the leftovers. Beans were my favorite. We ate corn on the cob when it was in season. Everyone except me loved wilted lettuce.

Corn bread and milk was the mainstay for supper (the evening meal). Sometimes we had fried squirrel. I was in high school before I ever tasted beef. We only had pork a few months out of the year. Remember, there was no electricity, no ice box. We had all kinds of canned fruit and vegetables. We had lots of fruit pies and cobblers. We made our own hominy. When I eat hominy today, it doesn't taste right. It has no taste of lye.

We sold our eggs to the hatchery, so we didn't have eggs or chicken very often. Until Mama had her chickens registered for the hatchery, our one source of regular income had come from selling our cream. The eggs were weighed and those failing to meet minimal weight standards were either eaten or sold to the Farmer's Exchange.

We also sold our male calves. Papa had a mill, blacksmith shop and saw rig that brought in some money. He also had a hot bed in one corner of the garden from which he sold plants ready to set out in the garden. None of these brought in much income. Another source of income was from the older children who held jobs. Without their financial support I don't know how we could have made it during the period from 1927–1935. They were very rough times.

All of us boys and some of the girls set rabbit traps during the winter months. At one time I had over twenty set out. The rabbits were hung in the smokehouse where they froze and the cream man picked them up when he picked up the cream. He sold them for us at the Farmer's Exchange for about ten to fifteen cents apiece and brought us the money on his next weekly cream trip. During the middle of winter I averaged about four rabbits a week, giving me a little spending money.

While we didn't eat the rabbits, we did eat the squirrels. Squirrel hunting was very popular. All the younger squirrels were fried; the old, tough ones were roasted like a chicken.

Opossum hunting, like trapping rabbits, was a source of income during hunting season. The only thing you needed was a good hunting dog. My cousin, Garry Marshall, had one the best opossum dogs in the country. He would only bark when he had one treed. Usually there would be about a half dozen in a hunting party. I went on only a few. I was always the youngest and, having the reputation of being a good tree climber, would have to climb the tree to shake the opossum out. They took the opossum away from the dog and put it in a gunny sack, to be killed and skinned after we got back home. Opossum furs sold for anywhere from twenty five cents to $1.25 each, depending on the size and condition of the fur. When you sold the furs you had to show you had a hunting license. We seldom had one, so we gave our furs to someone with a license to sell for us. Mom cooked some of the younger opossums; at the time, I thought they tasted good.

My father really loved fishing. About once or twice a year there would be a party of eight to ten people go on a two to three day fishing trip. My father furnished a large seine, a trot line and an apparatus to cook the fish over. One of the Kumbiers, who made their own wine, would bring along a couple gallons to bribe the farmer on whose property they were fishing. No kids were allowed.

Billy and I did a lot of fishing, but on a small scale. When the creek was running, we fished at the "Big Rock Piece." Otherwise, we fished on the creek near Hugh Ragland's place. Most of what we caught were small perch, tasty but full of bones.

News and Entertainment

WE HAD NO ELECTRICITY AT WALNUT GLEN, BUT WE HAD plenty of entertainment without it. We took two weekly papers: Capper's Weekly and the Kansas City Star. The main drawback was I couldn't get the pro boxing results until a couple of days after the fights. I was a boxing fan even at age twelve. For a period Harriet subscribed to the Jefferson City Daily News, but we dropped that after we got a radio.

Before our family had a radio, I used to go over to Ed Wilkerson's on Saturday nights to listen to the radio. It was actually a crystal set and we used ear phones to listen. When we finally got a radio at home, we used a car battery to power it. The one station we could get clear in the daytime was KWTO (Keep Watching the Ozarks) out of Springfield, Missouri. I could hear enough of the daytime St. Louis Cardinals' baseball games to sort of tantalize me, but the boxing matches at night came in clear.

We had a wind up record player that played 78 rpm records. Our favorites were the Carter Family and Jimmy Rodgers. Harriet and Ethel were always playing records when they were home. Donald and Mack also played records quite a bit.

All of us did a lot of reading. We kept books in a small, curtained off room at the top of the stairs. There was a small cot in this library of ours. Horatio Alger, James Oliver Curwood, Jack London, Ralph Conner, Mark Twain, and Zane

Grey were a few of the authors I remember. Hugh Gann, a friend of Felix, came over one Sunday while we were at Mabel's. When Hugh saw that no one was home, he grabbed a book from the library and began reading. By the time we got home it was dark. We did our chores and went to bed. Next morning, we were halfway through breakfast when Hugh came down the stairs, washed his hands, and sat down at the table. No one knew that he had been in the house overnight. Without saying a word Mama scrambled some more eggs for Hugh.

Dentistry and Medicine

WE SELDOM HAD NEED FOR A DOCTOR OR DENTIST, RELYING on home remedies instead.

The only time we used a dentist was when we had a tooth ache. It seemed that a tooth always began hurting in the middle of the night. Our home remedy was oil of cloves, salt in the cavity or a wad of cotton soaked in iodine and stuffed into a cavity.

My left front eye tooth was about to protrude. Dr. Smith, our family dentist, pulled a good tooth next to it. He then told me to press down on the eye tooth every time I thought about it for a couple of months. It worked. The empty space was quickly taken up by the tooth falling in place.

In the summer of 1937 or 1938 he charged me $17.00 for a bridge of one of my missing front teeth. The next time I saw him was in 1966. He was retired. I knocked on the door of his home. He said he knew that I was one of the Marshall boys, but he couldn't tell which one. I told him I wanted my $17.00 back because the bridge had lasted only fifteen years.

We seldom were sick. A doctor came to our house when Stanley was born and I saw a doctor in Conway once when I was coming down with the measles. Mom used turpentine and sugar on all cuts. Bandages were clean rags that had been hung out in the sun to be sterilized. For a cut, you put about a spoon of sugar on a bandage and pressed the sugared part against the cut. It always healed in four to five days when the bandage was removed. During the early spring Mom would make sassafras tea to "thin" out the blood for the summer. We drank this tea for three to four weeks.

Harry Talbot

THE TOWN OF PHILLIPSBURG HAD A POPULATION OF TWO hundred twelve when I was a freshman in the fall of 1935. Phillipsburg High School used to be a two-year high school, but had just graduated its first class of seniors in the spring of that year. There were twenty-two in my freshman class. Fourteen of those students plus three transfer students composed my graduating class of seventeen in 1939. Harry Talbot, the finest teacher I ever knew, was the superintendent. He was also the coach and taught math and English.

The grading system was E=excellent, S=superior, M=medium, I=inferior, and F=failure. We received grades every quarter. I had made all Es in freshman algebra. I received an E-minus on my first quarter in plane geometry my sophomore year. Harry Talbot shamed me by pointing to the minus sign and saying "You can do better than that." I made straight Es the rest of the year in plane geometry.

All four teachers my senior year were new. I'm not sure just what happened. I heard that someone on the PHS board saw Harry Talbot having a beer and recommended that he not be rehired, and, another teacher quit in protest. Perhaps it wasn't the fault of the new teachers, but whatever the reason, I really allowed my grades to slip my senior year.

I saw Harry Talbot twice after 1939. In November 1945, I stopped off for a brief visit with him at Camdenton, Missouri. He was the superintendent and coach at the high school there. I was on my way home to Jefferson City. Harry asked me to stop at the high school on my way back home and talk about my experiences as a POW. I chickened out. I didn't think I could talk to a large group like that. In April 1986, I visited Harry at Marshfield, Missouri. He was in bad health, but we had a good visit. After that we kept in touch until he died in 1990.

My Trip to Mississippi

IN THE SUMMER OF 1937 I WAS SIXTEEN. I HAD RECENTLY grown nearly two inches and gained a lot of weight, but not fat. I had put in the crops that year. I never felt I was much of a farmer, but with the exception of Donald, I did about as well as my older brothers. It was now late July and the crops were laid by. There would be several weeks before harvest time. Felix was in the Marine Corps and Donald was working in Kansas. Mama was visiting her mother in Ebenezer, Mississippi. My niece Selma (Mabel's daughter) was staying with us to do the cooking while Mama was gone.

For the first time in my life, I felt trapped—no money, no car, and no real future. Outside of going to Jefferson City twice, I had been nowhere. One Sunday, I decided that Billy and Stanley could do the milking, separating the milk and other chores. After everyone else went to bed that night, I packed a change of clothes and a tooth brush. I left a note for Papa telling him I was visiting some relatives in Mississippi and that I would be back in a few weeks.

I had no money other than a French coin. That night I walked to Highway 66 near Phillipsburg and slept by the side of a straw stack on one of the farms there. I caught a ride Monday morning to Springfield. I knew that the Springfield radio station had a fifteen minute "Man on the Street" program every weekday at noon. Each person interviewed received a box of cookies, so I walked to the location hoping to be interviewed. No luck!

I headed east on US-60 where I caught one short ride. It was midafternoon before I cleared the city limits of Springfield. I took advantage of a field of ripe tomatoes to satisfy my hunger pangs. I slept out in the open by the side of the road that night and woke up Tuesday morning damp with dew and starving. The first vehicle that came by was a man driving a horse trailer on his way to buy a horse from a farm near Willow Springs, Missouri. When we got there they were getting ready to sit down for breakfast of biscuits, sausage and gravy, which they shared. It was very, very good.

I managed very few rides the next sixty some miles to Thayer, Missouri. It was getting dark when I got there. I made friends with a seventeen year old who had just been fired by the railroad company. He had lied about his age. He warned me against hitchhiking through Arkansas, said they put hitchhikers on chain gangs. He told me there was a freight train going out about 1:00 a.m. Wednesday.

While I didn't believe his story about the chain gang, I did decide to try the freight train. I wasn't doing too well hitchhiking. Late that night we were joined by a regular hobo, who gave us some pointers, like never catch a moving freight at the rear end of the car. There is too much danger of falling between the cars. We caught our freight and were in Memphis, Tennessee before noon. I started hitchhiking south on what is now I-55, but caught very few rides. By this time I was really dirty, which didn't help. I gave up on hitchhiking and began riding local freights.

I got into Lexington about noon Friday, five days since leaving Walnut Glen. I had traded my French coin for a quarter and had a feast on a nickel loaf of bread and a six cent bottle of Royal Crown Cola. I finally located Aunt Mabel's on Friday afternoon. Everyone was dumbfounded when they saw me.

First, they drew a hot tub of water for me. What a mess I made of the bath tub by the time I got through washing. Aunt Mabel gave me a clean shirt and pair of jeans of my cousin's to put on. Saturday I got my own clothes back. She had washed and ironed them. We all went to a family gathering at Grandma's in Ebenezer on Sunday. Mama sure was surprised to see me. She was catching the bus back to Missouri the next day.

This was the first time I had met my grandmother. I liked her. She was an older version of my mother. Grandma said she would buy me a ticket home, that I was absolutely not hitchhiking or riding the freights back; but I was stubborn even then. We reached a compromise: I would not ride the freights; I would hitchhike. I stayed for a week, during which I did something that upset a lot of people.

I was out walking one day and came across a bunch of black boys playing rounders, just like what we played in Latimer School. They had a homemade baseball, bat and even a homemade glove for the catcher. They let me rotate in and we had a good time. We played baseball together for two or three days. When Grandma found out what I had been doing, she was extremely upset and put an end to my playing baseball with blacks.

Grandma gave me $5.00 when I headed back home. I was traveling first class with the $5.00. I got as far as Memphis the first day and went to see the movie *Topper*. It was so funny I sat through it twice. The second day I made it to Cairo, Illinois. I remember crossing one of the rivers on a simple ferry hooked to a cable attached to a site across the river and downstream. The force of the stream moved the ferry across. I slept by the

Peter, age 16 or 17, on Walnut Glen.

side of the road on the outskirts of Cairo, an old baseball cap laid over my face. I must have been very tired because when I woke the next morning I discovered that something had eaten the sweatband of my cap overnight.

That day I ran into the first girl hitchhiker I had seen. I had gotten a ride to a small town in Missouri, and when I got out of the car she was across the road, thumbing for a ride in the opposite direction from where I was headed. Once, she crossed the road to ask me if I had the makings for a cigarette.

I got home in about four days. Going to Mississippi meant a lot to me. It gave me a sense of accomplishment and boosted my self-confidence.

Basketball

WE HAD VERY LITTLE BASKETBALL AT LATIMER. PHILLIPS-burg High School had no gymnasium. What few games they played were on the opponents' home courts. I determined to make the PHS second team, and thus would make the team trips. Phillipsburg was such a small school that their basketball second team was made up of what was left after the first team's starting five.

When I got home from Mississippi, I fixed up a basketball court up above the chestnut trees beyond the house and yard. Papa made the backboards and mounted them on poles in the ground. He made basketball goals out of buggy tires. This didn't work out. The ground was too rough for much dribbling. The ball was always rolling down the hill. Finally we settled on the barn loft. We had a lot of two-on-two games. There was no out-of-bounds except when the ball went down the steps from the loft. Because of the limitations on the type of shots we could take this didn't help our shooting much, but it really conditioned me and made a good rebounder out of a 5'7" player. I think Coach Harry Talbot actually put me on the second team because I tried so hard.

I scored four points in our first game, which we lost by ten points. Much to my surprise I was named captain of the second team just before we played our second game at Conway. Our second team stayed intact the rest of the year. We beat Conway's second team easily. From the forward position I must have had eight to ten offensive rebounds, scoring nine points.

Our next opponent was North View, near Springfield. PHS's first and second teams won. I scored twenty points. The coach had me play the fourth quarter of the first team game. I didn't score or even shoot. The coach just wanted me to get a feel of playing in a varsity game.

During the early summer of 1939 I received the bad news that the contracts had not been renewed on any PHS teachers. I was angry and disappointed. PHS would have their first gymnasium. I had so looked forward to being a varsity starter on Coach Talbot's basketball team. So I decided to spend my senior year at Buffalo High School where Billy was attending. Word must have gotten around that I would be going to Buffalo. I was plowing corn in the lower basin when a new four-door Ford Sedan drove up. The new PHS coach Andrew Stottle got out of the car and joined me in the corn field. He was a young, very personable individual. He talked me into returning to Phillipsburg for my senior year.

I couldn't seem to relate to Coach Stottle on the basketball court. Overall, I had a mediocre season. The highlight for me was scoring the winning goal in double overtime in the first basketball game ever played indoors at Phillipsburg. PHS went 13 – 12 for our first year in the league. We had tried to cram four years into one and our athletic program had no money.

For all that, I really enjoyed playing basketball and I have been a big fan ever since.

Graduation

THE WEATHER WAS TERRIBLE ON GRADUATION NIGHT. THE creek was roaring from all the rain. It was still raining. I wrapped my new suit Edith had bought me in a water-tight bundle. With old clothes on I crossed the creek on the heavy cable that had been stretched across years before for emergency crossings. After crossing the creek, I walked a half mile in the rain to the Kumbiers. There I cleaned myself up and

Peter, age 18

changed into my suit. Harold Kumbier drove me to Phillipsburg. The graduation ceremonies went off without a hitch. I had some regret that I hadn't studied harder, especially the last two years. I was the first Marshall from Walnut Glen to graduate from high school. Jerome had quit school in his last semester. I think Felix had all his credits completed, but hadn't actually gotten his diploma. Our class motto was "Honors await at labor's gate."

Long, Hot Summer

I SUSPECT MY MOTHER CAME UP WITH THE IDEA NEAR THE END of my senior year that I would go to work for her half-brother, my Uncle Albert Rogers, in Skene, Mississippi. He had a small grocery store with a gas pump. He also sold kerosene and had a battery charger. No wages had been discussed, but it was taken for granted that I would work myself into a partnership in the store. Uncle Albert was about forty at the time.

I told all my friends I was going into the grocery business. Most of our graduating class had no idea what they would be doing. The Depression was still on. I was considered lucky to have a prospect.

When I left for Skene, Mississippi in mid-May 1939, I had about $7.00. I hitchhiked to Springfield and then caught a freight train. I didn't have as much fun traveling as I had two years earlier, but I was more efficient and arrived in Skene in three days.

Uncle Albert was nothing like I had imagined he would be. He was on the heavy side and a little sloppy in his dress. I liked him, but saw immediately that there was no future for me there. He cleaned out a little side room at the store for me to sleep in and to store my few belongings. I ate my meals with them. I was not paid while working there. Uncle Albert and his wife Ruth fought constantly. I guess the only thing that kept them together was their daughter, who was about seven.

Skene was located on the Mississippi Delta just a few miles from the river. It was hot and humid. I woke up each morning feeling like I had had no sleep. I was almost broke when I arrived at Skene, having spent more than I should have on the trip. Why I stayed the rest of the summer I don't know; maybe I thought I had to give it a chance.

I made no friends with anyone my own age, but I became friendly with some of the older men who traded at the store. Uncle Albert drank a lot. Mississippi was a dry state, but there were two stores in this town of about two hundred where liquor could be purchased. Apparently, these stores got a federal license and bought off the local law enforcement officials.

By late June, I really needed a haircut. I overheard someone say they had gone to this one barber shop and asked for a neck shave. It was almost like a haircut. The barber hadn't charged the guy, just asked him to come there for his next haircut. I decided to try that. Sure enough, I had my hair trimmed some with no charge. Sometime in July Mom sent me $1.00. I had not asked for it, but she must have sensed I was broke. I used the dollar for a haircut and a movie.

Mom had written she would be seeing me in August. Donald was driving her and Stanley to Mississippi for a visit. I had a long overdue talk with Uncle Albert. I told him I knew he was just barely hanging on to his store, that there was really not enough business for an extra hand. I told him I would be going back with Mom, Donald and Stanley. We parted friends. I felt sorry for him. I was disgusted with myself for wasting a summer. It had been miserable to say the least. I started hitchhiking to Ebenezer where my grandmother lived to catch my ride back home to Missouri.

On the Way Home

I SAID GOODBYE TO UNCLE ALBERT AND AUNT RUTH ON A Friday morning in August 1939. I had decided to go through Tchula and visit with Aunt Jo before going on to my grandmother's in Ebenezer, about 140 miles from Skene. I was in Greenwood walking to the southern edge of the town when I ran into a couple of young men about my age. They had been drinking. Maybe they could tell by my voice that I wasn't a southerner. One of them grabbed my bundle of belongings. When he refused to give them back, I slapped him as hard as I could. He came at me with both fists flying. I ducked all but one punch. I knew nothing about fighting but was a good wrestler. I got a waist lock on him and took him down. Then, astraddle his stomach, I pounded away at his face with both fists. His companion jumped on my back from behind. By this time, a bunch of Works Progress Administration workers had gathered around. They broke up the fight when it became two against one.

My nose was bleeding and my knuckles and elbows were skinned. My shirt was torn. One of the WPA workers invited me to go home with him that night at quitting time. He drove us in his Model T Ford. Their house had two rooms—a kitchen and a bedroom. They had an outdoor toilet. His wife mended my shirt. I put some disinfectant on my skinned knuckles and elbows. They took me with them to an old fashioned brush arbor revival meeting that night. I slept on the floor in their kitchen. Next morning he dropped me off on the edge of Greenwood. I was in Tchula by noon. I've often thought of that couple who took me in. They had almost nothing, but shared what little they had with me.

I had intended on staying only one night with Aunt Jo, but her oldest son, Junior, who was married, invited me to have dinner with him and his wife at her folks' farm that Sunday. Aunt Jo was real nice.

I had a very good visit over ten days or so with my grandparents in Ebenezer before Mom arrived. During that time, I drove Grandma and Grandpa everywhere except when we had to travel on a state highway. I had learned how to drive Donald's car, but didn't have a driver's license. They had an old Chevrolet with disk wheels.

My grandparents had a kerosene refrigerator and we had iced tea three times a day. Sometimes we had iced coffee. Mama, Donald, and Stanley arrived and stayed about five days. I'm not sure, but that may have been the last time Mama saw her mother. Except for a brief visit with Aunt Jo in 1967, it was the last time I saw any of Mama's relatives.

Donald was a good driver and we got home in a day and a half. Stanley sat on my lap as there was only one seat in the car.

Enlistment

I ENLISTED AT SPRINGFIELD NAVAL RECRUITING STATION IN October 1939 and passed my preliminary physical. In November I was sent to St. Louis for further physical exams and, after passing them, was sworn in and sent to the Naval Training Center at Great Lakes, Illinois. Early in my basic training I came down with cellulitis in my right foot and had to be hospitalized. This set me back a few weeks and I ended up in the same company as my brother Felix. After having served four years in the Marine Corps, he joined the navy just a few weeks after I had. Since Felix had previous military experience, he was made a "square knot Admiral" and assisted our chief petty officer in training us recruits.

I was an average recruit. I'll always remember how cold it was. It was so cold that most of our drilling was indoors. There was even an indoor firing range. I made the company wall scaling squad which competed with other companies once a month in athletic events. I played some as a substitute on my company's basketball team.

Upon completion of basic training we were given ten days' boot leave in February 1940 and drew our first pay. We were issued two coupon books worth $6.00 each, which was later deducted from our pay. One book could be used for luxuries, the other for necessities like shaving gear and toothpaste. This way each recruit had money saved for a roundtrip bus ticket home.

Peter in 1940 after hospital corps school.

While I was home on leave I had my nineteenth birthday. It was the last time I would see Walnut Glen Farm until late September 1945. I couldn't know at the time that it would also be the last time I would ever see my father. I regret to this day that, at age nineteen, I didn't hug him goodbye or say "I love you."

After boot leave, Felix and I reviewed the list of special schools in the Navy. I picked hospital corps school in San Diego; Felix picked radio school. We were promoted to Seaman second class ($36.00 a month).

Training wasn't too difficult, but I did have to study. After completing hospital corps school I was promoted to Hospital

Corpsman second class and assigned to the US Naval Hospital, San Diego, where I worked several months on the surgery ward. It was good experience and the work was satisfying. The worst part was being on call for special duty—Monday, Thursday and Friday one week, and the following week on Tuesday, Wednesday, Saturday and Sunday. (Special duty was from 9:00 p.m. to 12:30 am; 12:30 am to 3:30 am; or 3:30 am to 7:00 am). I had special duty about six times a month. This was in addition to regular duty.

Some patients, usually those under an oxygen tent, required a hospital corpsman by the bedside all through the night to check vital signs periodically. When on call it was my responsibility to check the special duty list. The worst thing was to have a patient die on your watch, which happened to me once. After calling the doctor to officially announce the patient dead, I had to follow a strict set of steps, including tying off the penis, stuffing the anus, etc. The last step was wheeling the body to the morgue.

In January 1941, I saw my name on the bulletin board, along with Woodrow Wilson Dunlap and Alfred Lee Daniels. We were to report to the destroyer base, San Diego on January 16 to await transportation to the USNH Guam. I had never heard of Guam. By this time I had made Hospital Corpsman first class ($54.00 a month) and had an allotment of $10.00 sent home to Mom each month. We were only at the destroyer base a few days before boarding the USS Chaumont, a naval transport, and embarking on a voyage to Guam.

1368 DAYS

Guam

A BOARD SHIP, ABOUT THREE WEEKS ALTOGETHER, I WAS IN charge of seeing that the patients in the sick bay were fed. I became pretty good at carrying all their food from the galley to the sick bay. I always ordered an extra ration so I could eat with the patients. We arrived on Guam in early February 1941.

Guam is C-shaped with the C partly straightened out. It is twenty eight miles long with an average width of eight miles. In 1941, the population was approximately 29,000, of which 19,000 in the capital, Agana. The native population was Chamorro. English was the official language, although everyone spoke Spanish or a form of it. The dominant religion was Catholicism.

There were no fortifications on Guam. It had a militia force of 400, poorly equipped and poorly trained. Guam was home port for three US naval vessels. The USS Penguin had a crew of about thirty or forty. The USS Goldstar had been on its way to the Philippines when the war broke out. The USS Barnes hadn't been to sea in years, serving as a training ship for mess attendants. The Barnes had a crew of eight. There were approximately 150 marines on Guam that served mainly as a police force. The naval hospital had a staff of about fifty, including five navy nurses. Altogether, the US military presence on the island was about 300.

The naval hospital was located in Agana. Captain W. T.

Lineberry, US Navy Medical Corps, was the medical officer in command of the naval hospital. Within the hospital compound, but separate from the naval hospital, was a private hospital for native patients who could afford to pay for their own medical care. It was staffed with one native doctor and with native nurses. When necessary, our naval doctors provided assistance.

I didn't drink before I came to Guam, but Daniels, Dunlap and I went on liberty together our first night on Guam and I had my first drink. In fact, I got drunk. When we got back to the hospital compound that night, they stood on either side of me, keeping me upright. When they let go of me to sign in, I fell flat on my face. My buddies then tucked me in my bunk. During the night I got sick and vomited all over myself and the bed. What a mess!

The next morning, February 5, we three reported to Dr. Van Peenen, the Officer on Duty. He needed two new people in the operating room to replace two that were headed stateside. Looking me in the eye, Dr. Van Peenen asked, "Which one of you got drunk last night?"

"I did sir." I replied.

He then said, "You are going on night duty in the ward."

There was a ward for native men and one for native women. While I was on night duty one of the patients had a heart attack. I immediately called Dr. Van Peenen, the OD that night. While waiting for him to arrive I laid out all the medications I thought he would need. Dr. Van Peenen seemed surprised that I had everything ready for him. On my last night of a month of working nights, Dr. Van Peenen greeted me as I came off duty. He said he wanted me to replace Dunlap as his OR technician. It felt good to have the surgeon specifically ask for me.

The OR crew consisted of surgeon Hubert J. Van Peenen, Lt. Commander (Medical Corps) USN; navy nurse Christenson; Chamorro nurse Delores "Lola" Deleon; a Chamorro student nurse; and four OR technicians: chief technician Clay Atwood, "Padre" Malone (he'd studied for the priesthood as a youngster), Alfred Daniels and me. OR technician duties included scrubbing up for operations, cleaning and sterilizing instruments, putting up sterile packs, and keeping the OR as spotless as possible at all times. Discipline was very strict. It was nearly a month before I was allowed to be on call alone in the OR. Finally I was given the green light by Dr. Van Peenen.

As luck would have it, my first day on call alone was a Sunday. My friend Al Mosher had been called in to the lab for an emergency urinalysis (for blood cells only), white blood count and differential. When I saw the results, I knew an emergency operation would be necessary. All the other OR technicians and the doctors, except Dr. Van Peenen, were on a fishing trip. Normally, in an emergency, all the other available OR technicians pitch in to give the one on call a hand. But, they were not available that Sunday. I knew that Jim Kelly, mate of the day, was an ex-OR technician, so I asked him for assistance. He said he would scrub, but that he wasn't familiar enough with our OR to circulate. I told him I would circulate. I filled him in on how Dr. Van Peenen liked to have the instruments handed to him. Dr. Van Peenen had Lola, the Chamorro nurse, assist him during the operation. Everything went like clockwork. Not one hitch. That one day made me as an OR technician.

During the year we had a little of everything in the OR, including some unusual operations: crushed skull, gunshot patient, thoracoplasty to partially collapse the lung of a patient with tuberculosis. Of all the assignments I had in the navy, working in the OR was by far the most interesting and enjoyable. Dr. Van Peenen was THE surgeon—the only one of the doctors on Guam whose specialty was surgery.

A few days before the outbreak of war with Japan, Lola boarded the Goldstar with two leper patients she was escorting to a leper colony in the Philippines. It was enroute when the war broke out.

I thought Guam was a beautiful place, a real South Sea island paradise. I was pleased to be there. It was a swell assignment. I learned to play tennis in my off duty hours. Some of the guys organized boxing matches. I think we all knew that war was coming, but in a state of wishful thinking, we chose to ignore the possibility. In early November 1941, we started digging L-shaped trenches on the hospital grounds for use in a bombing attack. Even knowing there was a strong possibility of war, it came as a surprise.

Invasion

ONDAY MORNING DECEMBER 8, 1941 (GUAM TIME) I BEGAN scrubbing for the first operation scheduled for 8:00 a.m.—Harley Odneal, a good friend of mine. Odie had had several light attacks of appendicitis. This Monday was supposed to be a light day for us in the OR so Dr. Van Peenen had scheduled to remove Odie's appendix before it gave him any more trouble. It was nearly 8:30, but no Odie. No Dr. Van Peenen either and he was never late. I had the instruments laid out and covered with a sterile towel. I was standing in a sterile gown, with sterile gloves on covered over with a sterile towel, wondering what in the world was going on.

Finally, at about 9:30, Dr. Van Peenen entered the OR. All the doctors had been in a meeting with Captain Lineberry. He said, "Operations are cancelled. Pearl Harbor has been bombed and Jap planes are overhead." As he spoke, enemy planes were bombing the marine barracks and a single plane machine gunned the hospital.

We immediately organized the wards for triage to have the worst cases go to Dr. Van Peenen with myself as his OR tech. Other doctors and OR techs would work the rest. Within thirty minutes the patients started pouring in. The first one was Jim Babb, whose his leg was blown apart. I've never worked so hard in all my life. Considering the circumstances, everything went very well.

By about 2:00 p.m. we had completed the surgeries on

the first batch of patients. The doctors left the OR to follow up on their patients and we OR techs and nurses worked feverishly to clean up, sterilize instruments, and put up more sterile supplies. We acted as central supply for all sterile supplies, including sterile liquids.

We were able to take a break sometime between 3:00 and 4:00 that afternoon. Sandwiches were sent up to us. Captain Lineberry dropped by and told us we were doing a great job. He then said we were needed and were not to leave the hospital compound under any conditions. About that time the next batch of patients were brought in. They were off the Penguin, which had been sunk. The sailors had been machine gunned while in the water. There were several intentional wounds. It was past midnight when we finished with these patients. Again we cleaned up and replenished our sterile supplies.

The second day of the war, December 9, was as bad as the first. I remember Frank Perry, one of 200 American civilians who had been sent to Guam to begin building military roads. He had a piece of shrapnel lodged against his spinal cord. Dr. Van Peenen agonized for a couple of minutes and then decided the best course of action under the existing circumstances was to leave the shrapnel as it was for a while. It could be removed at a later date.

We were caught up with our work and having coffee when Captain Lineberry dropped by and joined us. Then he said he had bad news. The Japanese were all over the island. He didn't mince words. He said by this time tomorrow we would all be prisoners of war or killed. I don't think I slept a wink that night. We all knew what the Japs had done in Shanghai and Nanking.

Captured

GUAM SURRENDERED DECEMBER 10, 1941. AFTER THE SURrender, a Japanese general and some aides entered the hospital compound. Captain Lineberry walked out to meet them. He saluted the general who returned the salute. The general then told Captain Lineberry to move all his patients and hospital personnel into one ward of the hospital. He also told him to limit the hospital personnel to twenty, including doctors, nurses, and hospital corpsmen. I was the only OR tech kept there. The others were taken to a cathedral on the north side of the plaza.

A couple of days later we twenty American men were taken to the middle of the hospital compound and lined up in a row. In front to our left was a manned machine gun. Directly in front of us was a manned machine gun. In front to our right was another. I had never been so scared in all my life. I can truthfully say I know how it feels just before you are put to death. I kept telling myself to die like a man and not show any fear. My heart was pounding. I could feel sweat running down my body. A Japanese officer gave us a long winded propaganda speech about the greatness of Imperial Japan. You could tell by the smirks on their faces they knew we expected to be executed and simply enjoyed watching us be afraid for our lives, but none of us broke down. We were enraged at their smug attitude.

I have absolutely no memory of anything after that until a month later.

On January 10, 1942 we were escorted outside the hospital compound to where the other POWs were being detained.

This was the first time we had been in contact with each other since the invasion. Our entire group consisted of less than 300 American military, nearly 200 American civilians, five navy nurses, a serviceman's wife and small baby, and five Spanish priests. (When all the other servicemen's wives were ordered back to the states shortly before the war, one wife was in a bad pregnancy. She was to have been sent back home after giving birth, but the invasion happened before a ship came.)

As we marched down the road toward Pita Navy Yard I learned what had happened to the POWs held outside the hospital compound. A group of about forty marines had surrendered together. After the surrender, one of the Japanese soldiers motioned to the marines to remove all their clothes. One either didn't understand or didn't move fast enough and was bayoneted through the gut. He gasped and sank to the ground without saying a word. Two headless marines had been found. Watches, rings, and all means of identification had been removed. For the first few days the POWs had been rationed one boiled potato per person per day. A native was caught slipping some food to the POWs through the fence. He was forced to dig his own grave in the middle of the POW compound, and then kneel with his head over the grave. With one stroke of a sword, a Japanese officer had decapitated the native and kicked his body into the grave. POWs who had been forced to watch were then ordered to fill in the grave.

Once, while still on the road to Pita Navy Yard, I was tempted to make a run for it. I was on the right hand side of five abreast and there was heavy brush along there. I thought maybe I wouldn't be missed for a while, but we were stopped and recounted every few minutes. I decided against trying to escape. The odds weren't too good.

We reached Pita Navy Yard and boarded the Argentina

Maru. The men were forced into the hold of the ship. I don't know where the women stayed. We didn't know where they were taking us. In the morning and at night, buckets of watery rice were lowered to us for food. Small groups at a time were allowed up the ladder to use the bathroom. I don't remember much else about the voyage. We arrived at the Japanese port of Todatsu on January 15.

Zentsuji

IT WAS DARK AND WE STAYED AT ANCHOR IN TODATSU FOR A number of hours. We hadn't been fed since receiving our watery rice ration that morning. The heat had been turned off on the ship. Wearing only our tropical clothes, it was not long before we were chilled to the bone and shivering uncontrollably. I don't remember if we were taken by train or buses to the nearby town of Zentsuji. We were taken to a building that had housed Russian POWs some forty years earlier. Here we were served a hot, weak vegetable soup. I was cold and hungry. It was hot and there was plenty of it, so it tasted really good to me. We were issued two blankets apiece and forty of us assigned to a room. The blankets were made of wood-fiber, thin and of poor quality, offering us little protection against the cold. Three of us pooled our blankets and slept together with all our clothes on.

The next morning and throughout the next week we got somewhat organized. The officers were separated from the enlisted men. The women were put in a separate room. Arrangements were made so they could go to the bathroom as a group while an American serviceman stood guard outside. Chief Boatswain's Mate Lane was put in charge of the enlisted men. Dr. Van Peenen and the other doctors set up a sick call routine. We were fed rice and weak soup twice a day, but we were allowed to use our own cooks. The day's food ration was given to the cooks one day at a time. There was a hot water bathroom we were allowed to use once a month.

The next week was indoctrination. Strict rules and regulations were posted everywhere. We were forced to sign statements that we would not try to escape. Those refusing to sign were put in a pen with no room to lie down. The bathroom was the ground. They were fed there also. They soon signed. The statement was meaningless because there was no way you could escape unless you had Asian features. Not one American POW escaped from the mainland of Japan.

Several Japanese scientists examined all our body areas, including scalps and arm pits. They even measured our flaccid penises. Why? I have no idea. Official photos were taken of all of us.

Finally, the enlisted men were put to work. As we left for work, each of us was given a rice ball for lunch. Our work was terracing the side of Osa Yama—a mountain. It was a long walk to the mountain, followed by a long and hard climb uphill. We leveled off an area, and then carried rocks to form a wall that held the soil in place at the edge. Then we moved up and start leveling off another area. It was exhausting work.

Sometime during the first half of 1942 arrangements were made to exchange the women for Japanese civilian POWs. Each of the five nurses took a list of one fifth of the names of the POWs to notify their next of kin of their present condition. We were all relieved to see the women safely returned home.

I got acquainted with people I hadn't really known before. There was Ed Howard, a sailor off the Penguin who was married to a native of Guam. They had a small son. Sewell Luften was a marine musician and had played in a band that performed in the park in front of the governor's mansion every Wednesday night. I had often listened to that band play. Clay-

POW photo taken by Japanese at Zentsuji

ton Atwood was adopted. Sgt. Vontom had just been selected to attend officer's candidate school when the war broke out. Carscallen and Arnett were amateur boxers and had held a boxing match on Guam. Tony Iannarelli had acted as trainer for Carscallen and hadn't allowed him to drink a beer for an entire month. After the fight that ended in a draw, all three men went drinking together.

We were allowed to write home.

From the time we were taken prisoner there were two constants for me—hunger and humiliation. I think this was true for every American POW. I was always hungry. This can gnaw on you after a while. From day one the Japanese humiliated us in every way possible. I suppose that was designed to break our spirit.

Just as we were getting used to the routine at Zentsuji, 150 of us were moved to Osaka without prior notice. I didn't even get a chance to say goodbye to friends I never expected to see again. CBM Sanders was the POW in charge of this 150. There was one doctor among us, but I don't remember his name.

Osaka Stadium Camp

THE BOAT RIDE TO OSAKA TOOK ABOUT TWENTY FOUR HOURS. One incident on the boat I remember. I was using the urinal when a middle aged Japanese woman walked up to the urinal, turned around, bent over and let fly. I thought if it doesn't bother her, it won't bother me. We reached Osaka on June 8, 1942 and were marched to the basement of a stadium. For the next couple of months we lived under the stadium stands.

The quarters were terrible. Musty. Not enough ventilation. We had one set of old Japanese uniforms for clothing. We worked long hours as stevedores on the docks. We got only two days off a month and were harassed on those days. We weren't used to that type of work, and at first our muscles were very sore. Soon our unwashed-many-times-sweat-stained trousers could nearly stand alone. We were taken to work by a different route each day so more civilians could see us. They yelled and spit on us and threw things as we passed. Some who spoke English yelled at us that Japanese soldiers would never surrender.

We got used to the work and got stronger. When we were handling foodstuff we managed somehow to get some food. I remember unloading a shipment of dried coconut that had been shipped in straw bags. It was easy to tear a small hole in a bag and help ourselves to chunks of coconut. They were tasty and filling, but unfortunately acted as laxatives. We had the runs for days.

There were a few accidents, including some that were fatal. During the time we were in the stadium, our doctor was sent back to Zentsuji along with two or three patients that were in no shape to work. The doctor didn't return.

During those months in the Osaka stadium quarters I developed a survival plan of sorts. It was now obvious that we were going to be POWs for one or more years to come. I decided to make myself as invisible as possible and never ask for anything from the Japanese such as food, clothing or cigarettes. When anything went wrong, the Japanese always took it out on some POW that looked familiar to them. I would never do anything that reflected negatively on the United States. That may sound corny, but it was important to me, and I am sure it was to the others. We had to be positive about something. There is nothing glamorous about being a prisoner of war. When war broke out I followed orders to the letter. The only time I could have made an attempt to escape would have been on the march from Agana to the Pita Navy Yard. I am almost certain that would have been suicide. But, if I could survive being a POW with honor, I would be accomplishing something. I would conduct myself in such a way as to make the Japanese remember Americans as being brave honorable people. I could feel good about myself.

We were getting used to the hard work. The noon ration of a rice ball plus other food tidbits we could scrounge helped build up our strength. After a while we were taken to work the quickest way possible. The people got used to seeing us going and coming from work and began pretty much to leave us alone.

We were able to scrounge bits and pieces of cloth. Some POWs, like Reid Harrod, had small sewing kits. After he made himself a couple of G-strings to work in, I borrowed his kit and made myself a couple of G-strings. During the lunch break we could wash our trousers in sea water while we worked in our G-strings. Eventually, we developed a routine: wear our clean trousers to work, change into a G-string, wash ourselves in sea water at the end of the day and put our clean trousers back on. I was proud of my efforts to stay clean and maintain navy discipline.

Osaka POW Camp Number 1

ABOUT THE FIRST OF OCTOBER 1942 OUR GROUP WAS SPLIT, again without prior notice. Eighty men were sent to another POW camp outside Osaka. A few days later, the rest—about sixty-six of us—were moved to the new main camp in Osaka, built just for prisoners. This camp became Osaka POW Camp Number 1. It was the headquarters POW camp for all POW camps in the Osaka area. As you entered the camp, there was a guard house on the left and the guards' living quarters on the right. Behind that was the main building for the prisoners. It had six bay rooms with a central corridor. The entire camp could hold 396 prisoners.

As you entered the POW compound there was a guard house to your immediate left. To your immediate right was a sick bay of sorts. There was a cobbler shop. Shoes or lack of shoes was becoming a problem. A sailor from Guam became our cobbler. There was a warehouse. Then you came to six rooms, which were really bays, three on either side of a four foot walkway. Each of the three rooms made up a single building. A common wall separated Room 1 from Room 3. Another common wall separated Room 3 from Room 5. Across the way Room 2 had a common wall with Room 4. Room 4 had a common wall with Room 6. The toilets were located in that general area. At one end of the rows of spigots was a boiler with two spigots. This was where we got hot water for tea and shaving. There was a narrow walkway on one side of Room 5. Those in Rooms 2, 4, and 6 had to use the walkway to get to the toilets, hot water for tea, etc. You can see it was a big advantage being in Rooms 1, 3, and 5.

Those of us from the Osaka stadium were initially moved into Room 1. Chief Boatswain's Mate Sanders was in charge of our group. There was no doctor. We were put on a work detail as usual the next day.

Within a couple of weeks several nationalities of POWs poured in. There were soldiers, sailors, and marines from Wake Island and the Philippines. There were Englishmen from Singapore. There were crews off English and American merchant vessels that had been sunk by German raiders. The Germans turned any prisoners over to Japan, the closest place to get rid of them. The English ship crews included Chinese and Indians. Our rooms filled in a hurry. Some had to be sent to another POW camp.

There was a transition period of getting organized again. The Japanese divided us so that one bay was all army, another navy, another marines. There was also an all English room and a room containing a hodgepodge of Indians, Chinese, and leftover Americans and Englishmen. Each room elected a room honcho. Our honcho was George Maloof. He was a good choice. Not only was he an eternal optimist, but he could recite poetry, including most of Robert Service's works. He was very well liked and well respected by everyone. He really was one of the nicest men I've ever known.

CBM Sanders was the POW in charge of the camp. The Japanese gave him orders, which he relayed to each of the room honchos, who in turn gave the orders to their rooms.

Each bay room held sixty-six prisoners. There were three shelves on either side with eleven straw sleeping mats on each shelf. Each sleeping mat was between two and three feet wide and about six feet long. The first shelf was about a foot off the floor. The second shelf was three to four feet above the first. The top shelf was about the same distance from the middle shelf. On the top shelf you could stand up and stretch; however, there was a disadvantage to the top shelf. When the charcoal burner was lit, the gaseous fumes rose to the top. We suffered severe headaches from the fumes. Fortunately for us on top, the month's supply of charcoal only lasted a couple of days. We had two blankets each and a small pillow stuffed with barley chaff or something like that. I would wake up at night and the side of my head lying on the pillow would be numb. We slept head to toe so as not to cough in anyone's face.

I was on the top shelf. To my immediate left was Mosher. To his immediate left was Salisbury. To my immediate right was Schwab. To his right was Odneal. To Odneal's right was Harrod. The six of us maintained those positions for two years and nine months.

A loner couldn't survive in a POW camp. We formed into groups of two, three, and even four. I was in a group with Albert Schwab and Alfred Mosher. I couldn't have asked to be associated with two nicer people. Anything of any value, usually food or soap, obtained by anyone in my group was split three ways.

Odneal and Harrod formed a twosome. Salisbury teamed up with a sailor from the Penguin. On the top shelf across from me was a twosome of Jim Darden and Jimmy Muldrow, both seamen. Darden was captured on Wake Island. Muldrow was a member of a gun crew on a ship sunk by the Germans. Every finger on both of Muldrow's hands had been broken or badly damaged by shrapnel, but somehow he seemed to manage as well as anyone. Jimmy was the youngest in the room, having joined the navy after Pearl Harbor.

Here's a typical day. The room honcho saw that everyone was awake by 5:30 a.m. We were fed at about 6:15. The food was brought in buckets. Each person had his own eating utensils. The order to fall out for work came at about 7:15. We lined up in rows outside the POW compound. The last dozen or so to fall in line were pounded with canes on their backs. It didn't matter how fast you lined up, you were always pounded if you were in the last few. This delighted the Japanese sergeant who dished out the pounding. The Americans referred to him as the Straffer; the British as Sergeant Markoff (from the movie *Beau Geste*). A representative from each Japanese company using our labor was present. Some work groups were permanent and the same POWs worked for that company every day. Others would request so many men. Any leftover POWs were forced on the largest group, but usually there weren't enough men to fill the requests.

We got a ten minute break in the morning, usually thirty minutes for lunch, and a ten minute break in the afternoon. The company using us provided lunch, usually some rice cooked with soybeans or barley. Often, there was also some dried fish, seaweed, or pickled daikon. The food tasted good, but was never enough. We were always hungry. I spent years being hungry even after I had just eaten.

We always got back to our camp about dark. The first one in my threesome to return lined up for the hot water spigot for our hot tea. Sometimes we three worked on the same detail, so then we took turns getting in line for the hot water. The Japanese gave us green tea. While the tea was brewing we washed up the best we could.

Then came the best time of the day. It was a ritual. The one who lined up for the hot water was the host. He poured the tea and then announced it was ready. We sipped tea facing each other, usually not saying a word. It was fellowship. Sometimes it felt like a religious experience. All over the room you saw twosomes, trios, and groups of four sipping their tea. We usually finished just before the evening meal was brought in.

Sometimes there were announcements by our room honcho. We were mustered in at 8:00 p.m. each day. A Japanese officer accompanied by a guard and CBM Sanders would enter the room. Maloof, our room honcho, would shout attention in Japanese. Then, also in Japanese, he would shout count off: ichi, ni, san, etc. You knew ahead of time what your number would be. You were to remain sitting at attention until all six rooms had been mustered in. Then Sanders would shout all clear. The room honchos would relay the all clear to their rooms. Lights went out at 9:00 PM.

The toilets had a slit about six inches wide that you straddled when you squatted. You didn't sit down. You squatted. One night a person in Room 5 had diarrhea. As soon as his room was mustered in, he slipped out and was squatting on the last toilet. In the meantime a person in Room 6 had to pee in the worst way. The green tea was getting to him. When the mustering party left his room he dashed down the passageway on the side of Room 5. The lights partially blinded him and he let fly when he was about five feet away from the toilet. He urinated all over the poor guy squatting. It was kind of funny to everyone except the two involved. No one got angry.

We had a great Christmas in 1942. We didn't get an extra day off from work, but one of our two days off for December occurred on Christmas Day. Not only were we left alone, but we each received a Red Cross food parcel box. There was a giant chocolate bar, can of corn beef, sweet cream butter, sardines, powdered milk, and I don't recall what else. The first thing I ate was several spoons of powdered milk. For a few days I had all I wanted to eat, and then the Red Cross box was empty. That was the only Christmas I remember while a POW.

New POWs brought us bad news. Except for Midway, it seemed the Japanese had been successful in every war venture against the United States. We were in it for the long haul. They told us of new acts of Japanese brutality, the worst being the formation of Blood Brothers, practiced in the camps in the Philippines where escapees could find help from the natives. The Japanese divided the POWs into groups of ten. If one escaped, the other nine were executed. We also heard details of the Bataan Death March, where POWs not able to keep up were bayoneted on the spot.

Some work details were worse than others. The one I hated most was Chuba Goon (at least that how it sounded), a lumber yard. When a truck arrived, the POWs carried lumber from different stacks to fill an order. The soil was sandy and carrying lumber in that sand really sapped your strength. I was carrying a load when a Japanese civilian hit me on the back of my head, causing me to drop to my knees and spill my load. I decided my best course of action was to pretend to be unconscious. He kicked me several times in the ribs, but fortunately for me he was wearing rubber type shoes. It hurt, but I suffered no broken ribs. After the kicking stopped and I heard him walk away, I looked up. I saw a guard staring at me. I know he must have seen the attack. I got up, reloaded the lumber on my shoulder and that was the end of that. I was humiliated and hurt physically, but it was nothing serious, and I was still alive.

There was one detail I almost enjoyed. It was at a nail

factory. I worked there for about eight months in 1943. An elderly Japanese workman, I would guess about seventy years old, nailed tops onto kegs of nails, which I then stacked according to nail size. When the workman saw that I understood what he wanted me to do, he left me alone. When he rested he motioned for me to take a rest; the same for lunch. In the afternoon break he always offered me a cigarette. I accepted it and nodded my thanks. We never spoke to each other during the eight months I worked there. However, after a few weeks he would greet me with a smile when I arrived at work. I would return his smile. He was one of two Japanese I think might have remembered me as a person. He impressed me and I think I impressed him.

By now we had written a few letters and had received a few letters. We were told what we could and could not write.

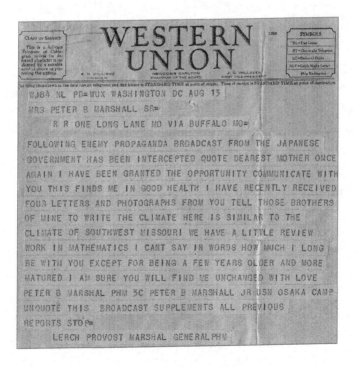

The basement of the stadium where we stayed when we first arrived in Osaka had been converted into a POW hospital. Only about ten percent of the patients survived a stay there. Of course, those sent there were already half dead.

Our camp had no doctor. Clayton Atwood, Pharmacist Mate second class was in charge of the sick bay and held sick call. The Japanese allowed only so many POWs to be sick at one time. Atwood had to decide who was too sick to work, or who was so bad off that they should go to the POW hospital. It was a difficult decision that a doctor should make. Many POWs shouldn't have worked in the condition they were in, but dared not let anyone know they were sick for fear of being sent to the POW hospital.

I had a terrible tooth ache one night. Aspirin, the only thing we had for pain, had no effect on the tooth ache. I didn't know Atwood had some morphine. He had been working in the pharmacy when Guam surrendered and managed to take several vials with him when he left the hospital. He saved them for emergencies. I guess he felt sorry for me because he gave me a shot of the precious morphine. The next morning my jaw was swollen to twice its normal size. I was taken to a Japanese dentist, who did a nice job of pulling the bad tooth. Nevertheless, I thought it was very dangerous to pull my tooth while the jaw was still swollen the way it was. I missed only half a day of work.

Mostly we were used as stevedores, unloading ships onto barges. We unloaded to docks, and from the docks to train cars or trucks. We unloaded iron ore from barges into train cars. The hardest work we had to do was to carry loads on our shoulders from the docks to train cars. I spent many days carrying 100 kilo bags (roughly 220 pounds.) The tallest and strongest were the loaders. They actually had the most difficult jobs.

With a short cargo hook in each hand, the two loaders, one on each end of the bag, would lift the bag. You bent down as much as you could until they placed the bag on your back. The loaders kept lifting until you stood up straight before they removed their hooks. You quickly learned the easiest way to carry 220 pounds.

I think we laborers had it twice as good as the officers, who didn't have to work. Between the lunch we were given and food we stole while working, we were better fed. During the day we were too busy to be bored. At night we were too tired to be bored.

There were no more Red Cross parcels. I know some had been sent, but I'm certain the Japanese kept them for themselves.

The POWs became expert at stealing food from the work place and bringing it into the camp. There was a shortage of food for the Japanese people as the war went on and on, and the guards began searching us more thoroughly as we returned to camp from a job. Periodically we were forced to completely strip down before entering camp. Even the G-string was no longer a safe place to sneak in stolen food. Men found with stolen food were forced to bend over and were beaten with light bamboo canes which split and grabbed the flesh. They screamed from the pain. Their rear ends were in shreds afterwards. I was either too cautious or too much of a coward to ever get caught stealing food. Somewhere along the way I had decided the risks outweighed the benefits.

We were losing two to three men a week from our camp. As a man got too sick to work, he was sent to the POW hospital, and that was the last you ever saw of them. My room suffered the least losses, I am almost certain. We had about a dozen pharmacist mates in our room and George Maloof, our room honcho, was an outstanding man. I think we just took better care of each other.

Toward the end of 1943 tempers flared up more than usual. Sane heads prevented most fights, but some happened before they could be stopped. One night a POW climbing to his top shelf got some mud on someone's mat on the second shelf. That person said something about it, and then we heard a sickening sound of a nose being busted. Both men were sorry afterwards.

Odneal and Harrod had been close friends for two years on Guam, but they almost came to blows one night. The rest of us grabbed them before either could throw a punch. They both cooled off right away. Once in a while there would be two guys who insisted on punching it out. If they were about the same size we let them fight in the area where the toilets and water spigots were. Someone acted as referee, usually "Battler" Ryan, a former professional boxer. When one was hurt or one obviously getting the better of the other, the referee broke up the fight. I never watched any of the fights myself.

There was absolutely no privacy, something you never quite got used to it. Serious teasing was forbidden. No way did you want to increase the tension or make someone feel worse than they already did. You had to learn to overlook everyone's idiosyncrasies. For example, Mosher couldn't stand to eat out of the same canteen he shaved out of, so I let him use mine to shave out of. You really had to learn to give and take.

People with expertise surfaced over time. Boxing disputes were settled by "Battler" Ryan. Sewell Luftin was the expert on music. He had played in the Marine Band and tried to teach us an appreciation of music. A former Australian school teacher was the expert on languages.

By now all of us knew most everybody in the camp.

MAY 1, 1944

Dearest Mother, PaPa + rest of family
I'm still O.K. Have received
several letters from you + Ethel. Also
received your other pAckage. Am
wearing the underwear, sox, + shoes now.
It's hard to keep faith in our Country
at time but I relize that wars Aren't
won over night
The letters I got have done me more
good than Anything else could do.
Tell those "Men of War" brothers of
mine I would like to be with them.
Would like to see Stanley's graduation
exercises. Stanley is to go on to college.
I'll put up the money when I get bAck
                            love,
                            Peter B. Marshall

Letter received. March - 17 - 1945

Letter from Peter to his family, May 1944

Jimmy Muldrow with his mangled hands. A crew member
off a US merchant ship had part of his face missing. He had
to hold what was left of his nose in order to draw on a cigarette. A marine sergeant with an improperly set bone in his
leg walked around with one leg several inches shorter than

the other. There was an Englishman off a British merchant ship who was its sole survivor. The German captain of the raider that sank his ship only picked up one survivor of each ship he sank. There was a Spanish captain in the loyalist army that didn't dare return to Spain. A small group of Indians faithfully practiced their religion. Each carried a small can of water with them when they used the toilet. In his faith he could be the father of the Christ yet to come, therefore his genitals must always be clean.

We got through the winter of 1943-44. We really began to notice the heat in the summer of 1944. The large logs in our building had cracks where bed bugs holed up. I would wake up at night and feel sweat running off my body. Or was it bed bugs? They were all over the place.

In the fall of 1944 I was on a work detail for several weeks with a marine, Supply Sergeant Knighten. For some reason we hit it right off and became close friends. He developed respiratory problems, and after a few days was sent to the POW hospital. I never expected to see him again. He returned to our camp after about a month, but he wasn't the same person. I hardly knew him. He was like a zombie. His eyes looked dead. He wouldn't speak except to beg not to be sent back to that hospital. Within a couple of weeks he was sent back and this time he died.

Some people have eyes that are full of expression. There was a sailor with eyes like that on the top shelf across from me. He suffered from almost every malady and his condition worsened each day. He lapsed into a coma from which he never recovered. He too died in the POW hospital. He was so starved by the time he died that one of his eyes popped out of its socket. The thought horrifies me to this day.

I began having breathing problems and gradually lost my

strength. One night I couldn't climb to the top shelf after coming in from a work detail. Mo and Schwab helped me up on my shelf, and then one of them notified Atwood in the sick bay. I was put on the official sick list. By this time we finally had a doctor in our camp. He tapped me on my chest and said he thought my pleural cavity was full of fluid, thus partially collapsing my lung. With a large needle and syringe the doctor drew off a great amount of fluid. However, that only gave me temporary relief while the sac filled up again. We had some sulfa drugs sent by the Red Cross and I was given sulfathiazole. This made me vomit and I became dehydrated. The doctor tried sulfadiazine, which worked, but I couldn't lie down. I had to sit up to be able to breathe.

I was terrified of being sent to the POW hospital. Fortunately, I was allowed to stay in the dispensary, although I don't know why. Maybe it was because Atwood was a friend of mine that I wasn't sent to the POW hospital right away. About the third morning in the dispensary, the patient next to me died. I knew him well. He was from the bottom shelf across from me. We had just received a semi-sweet roll for our morning meal. He died before he had a chance to eat it. Atwood gave the roll to me. I was very hungry, but I couldn't eat it. It belonged to a dead man. In a few days I said I was ready for a work detail. I really wasn't, but was too afraid of being sent to the POW hospital. Every breath I took hurt. Mo and Schwab had to help me to the top shelf every evening for a couple of weeks. They wouldn't let me take my turn at washing our eating utensils, nor allow me to stand in line for hot water for our tea. I also received help from Odneal and Harrod. Gradually, over six weeks, I began to improve almost back to my old self.

1944 ended up not being my best year, but I was still alive.

1945

IN FEBRUARY 1945 I HAD AN ACCIDENT THAT COULD WELL have been fatal. It hadn't been that long since I had been really sick. We took a lunch break from unloading iron off a barge. Being nearly empty, it was sitting high in the water, the top even with the dock. I was talking with Mosher as we returned to work. I thought I was stepping onto the barge when a wave pulled it away from the dock. I fell a long way before hitting the water. The barge being nearly empty saved me. There were several feet of clearance at the water level between the barge and the dock, making it possible for me to climb out. After seeing I was okay, everyone had a big laugh. The Japanese guard helped me build a small fire. I took off my shoes and socks, but kept on my shirt and trousers. I was back to work within an hour. I didn't even catch a cold from the incident.

One of the Japanese guards seemed to like me. He acted like a shell-shocked veteran. I heard one of the Japanese yell "baca" at him. In Japanese that can mean crazy, stupid, or something similar. I felt sorry for him and maybe he sensed that. He gave me the book *The Road Back* written by Erich Maria Remarque, who also wrote *All Quiet on the Western Front*.

1945 was a bad year for Japan. Early in the year a tidal wave damaged the sea wall and certain areas in Osaka. This was followed by an earthquake that really scared us POWs, but didn't do too much damage. We were on a work detail when the earthquake hit. There were large cracks in the earth. We ran and jumped into an empty barge.

In March there was an air raid that lasted several hours. No bombs hit our camp, but several came close. A single B-29 Ranger we dubbed the *Lone Ranger* flew over our camp almost nightly just before muster. After muster, every POW who was number twenty nine from his room was taken to the guard house. There they were forced to kneel with their shins resting on the groove of the sliding doors of the guard house while holding a partially filled bucket of water out in front of them.

We were handling truck fuel on a job one day. It was mostly alcohol and some of the POWs started drinking it. One secreted a bottle in his G-string and snuck it back into camp where he drank some before muster. During muster he took a swing at the Japanese officer who simply stepped back. The drunken POW fell flat on his face. The officer beat the guy almost to death, and then announced he would be shot at sunrise. I guess the camp commander overruled his officer because he wasn't shot.

On June 1, 1945 we were on the same work detail where the earth had cracked during the quake when all hell broke loose. About 10:00 a.m. I heard a droning overhead and looked up. I spotted vapor trails before I saw the B-29s, so many of them, perhaps a dozen in the first group. We weren't scared initially, but then bombs started falling and we all hit the dirt. One bomb landed so close to me it kicked sand on me, but it didn't go off. I think it was filled with inflammable fluid. Before the next wave of planes appeared, the eight of us crawled under some heavy machinery. After the second round of bombing, someone said if an incendiary bomb fell on our group we would all catch on fire, so we jumped in the bay. The earthquake earlier in the year had loosened some chunks of concrete on the sea wall, giving us a protective ledge to get under. We were in about three and a half feet of water. Then someone worried aloud that if a high explosive were dropped anywhere close, the ledge would cave in, crushing us. In between waves of bombing we dragged over some steel bars to brace the overhanging concrete ledge. It took us a while, but we finally got it right.

There was an engineer off one of the ships sunk by the bombs that refused to leave our previous safety spot under the heavy machinery. An incendiary bomb landed close to him and set him on fire. Even his beard was burning. We jumped up from our area of safety and threw him in the bay. Others still in the bay dragged him to our little cove. He was conscious, but in terrible shock. We had nothing to treat him with. We could only make sure he didn't drown himself before the air raid was over.

The raid lasted about four hours. Our guard had disappeared. We rigged a stretcher from a couple of poles and straw mats and were ready to start back to our camp when a small boat showed up. One of the bridges was burned out, so we returned to camp in the boat. Our camp was burned to the ground. Someone had salvaged my toothbrush and spoon. We were trucked to some warehouses and factory buildings on the other side of Osaka. I learned later that the engineer survived although I never saw him again.

We were in these temporary quarters nearly three weeks. I received a letter from home. Mom didn't mention Papa in her letter so I was pretty sure Papa had died. We were bombed every day. During one raid I was lying against the side of a concrete building when I heard a moan. It came from Mosher, who was lying against the concrete around the corner from me. I thought to myself I wasn't the only one who was scared.

One night after dark we were loaded onto a train and sent to Fushiki, a port on the west coast of the main island of Honshu. Osaka was burning when the train left. We were packed in this train like sardines in a can. You could hardly move. There was one toilet, but most of us, including myself, never made it to the toilet. We all reeked of urine and worse. Sometime during the next afternoon we arrived at Fushiki.

We were a mess. The new camp was a mess and was poorly organized. People were dying all over the place, two or three a week from dysentery and other related diseases. I could hardly wait for a work detail just to get away from the camp. We worked as stevedores again, cleaning out the bilges of a ship. I worked barefooted because I wanted my shoes to last another winter, although I began to wonder how many of us would be alive after the coming winter. It would be much colder here than in Osaka. We handled no food on our work details, so we couldn't steal to supplement our meager rations. The guards and Japanese civilians were surly.

Japan Surrenders

AUGUST 16, 1945 WE WERE ON A WORK DETAIL WHEN SUDDENLY all the Japanese workers gathered around the radio. A few minutes later our guard took us back to camp and then he took off. The only guard remaining was a Japanese sergeant who spoke English. He had been pretty decent to us. He told us the Allies and Japan were talking peace terms, that the war was over and he would help us in any way he could. We asked for guns, food, and a radio, which he supplied. We set up our own guard just inside the POW compound. We wanted to keep our people inside. No one was celebrating; we were all apprehensive. Nobody knew where we were. We found an English speaking channel on the radio, an international Red Cross station. We heard that all POW camps were urged to paint large POW signs on our buildings for aerial spotting. We did just that.

A few days later, about August 23, an American plane spotted our camp. He flew down low and dropped a small bundle containing four packs of cigarettes and a note. The note said that the location of our camp had been radioed back to headquarters and that food and cigarettes would be parachuted to us in a couple of days. From that day on, an American plane circled our camp each day. This made us feel more secure. True to the pilot's word, K-rations and cigarettes galore were parachuted down to us. I remember eating powdered milk by the spoonful from the first K-rations.

The first night after the food and cigarettes were dropped, someone built a small fire in the middle of the POW compound. That fire was kept going during the rest of our stay there. Parts of the building were ripped off for fuel. Any time of the night there was a gang around the fire eating, smoking, and talking.

On the afternoon of September 2, a USAF colonel and a reporter from *Yank* magazine drove up in a Japanese truck. Japan had signed the surrender documents. The colonel was in charge of transporting POWs from their various camps. He told us about the atomic bomb. The reporter took pictures of several POWs.

We boarded a Japanese train September 6. Armed Japanese military police escorted us. I believe they were the only members of the Japanese military allowed to retain arms. The boarding of the train was proceeding smoothly when the *Yank* magazine reporter did what I considered to be a cruel and stupid thing. He threw out handfuls of army hardtack biscuits and took pictures of Japanese children picking them up and eating them. We POWs had worked so hard portraying Americans as brave, upright people only to have someone like the reporter pull a stunt like that. I never tried to obtain the issue of *Yank* with pictures of our camp. After that incident I was no longer interested.

A plane flew cover for our train and if we were held up for any unexplained reason, the pilot signaled, "Do you need help?" We gathered outside and stood in formation of the word "NO." Then he wagged his wings in understanding.

We made it into Tokyo the next afternoon. We were now officially in American hands once again. We boarded a hospital ship where we cleaned up, showered and shaved. Then we were sent aboard a combat ship. We were fed enormous amounts of food and treated like heroes while aboard ship. It was good to sleep on a bed again after so many years on the hard shelves.

Those of us from Guam had been POWs for 1368 days.

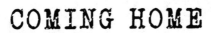

COMING HOME

POWs arriving in Norman, Oklahoma.
Peter is the fourth from the left.

The Trip Home

WE LEFT TOKYO BY A NAVY C-54 ON THE MORNING OF SEPtember 8, 1945. We cruised at about 180 mph, arriving at Guam ten hours later. It was so built up that I couldn't tell what part of the island we were on. We arrived long after dark and were taken directly to a mess hall. A navy commander was my waiter! I slept that night on a hospital bed. First thing after breakfast on September 9, I was interviewed by naval intelligence. I gave names and descriptions of four Japanese officers who had been unusually cruel. Then we took off for Kwajalein in the Marshall Islands. We arrived sometime past midnight, refueled the plane, stocked up with beer, and then took off again, this time for Pearl Harbor. I think we spent two nights and one day there and I was able to draw three months' pay.

Next stop was the naval base in Oakland California. I know we arrived on September 12, five days after leaving Tokyo, after gaining a day crossing the international dateline. It was my first time on American soil in four years and seven months. Upon arriving we were given a free phone call. I called my sister Edith because Mom had no phone. I told her I was okay. I asked about the family and learned that Papa was dead. Mosher and I went out on liberty together. We took it pretty easy. I had been sort of numb ever since August 16. I was promoted to pharmacist mate second class.

We were in Oakland for two days being examined and

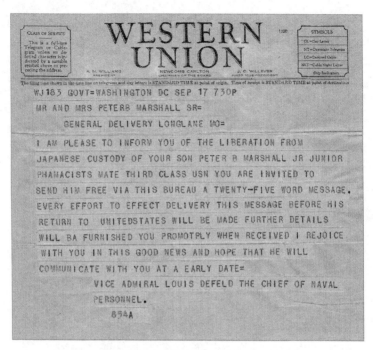

WESTERN UNION

CLASS OF SERVICE
This is a full-rate Telegram or Cablegram unless its deferred character is indicated by a suitable symbol above or preceding the address.

A. N. WILLIAMS PRESIDENT
NEWCOMB CARLTON CHAIRMAN OF THE BOARD
J. C. WILLEVER FIRST VICE-PRESIDENT

1120

SYMBOLS
DL=Day Letter
NT=Overnight Telegram
LC=Deferred Cable
NLT=Cable Night Letter
Ship Radiogram

The filing time shown in the date line on telegrams and day letters is STANDARD TIME at point of origin. Time of receipt is STANDARD TIME at point of destination

WJ183 GOVT=WASHINGTON DC SEP 17 730P

MR AND MRS PETERB MARSHALL SR=

    GENERAL DELIVERY LONGLANE MO=

I AM PLEASE TO INFORM YOU OF THE LIBERATION FROM
JAPANESE CUSTODY OF YOUR SON PETER B MARSHALL JR JUNIOR
PHAMACISTS MATE THIRD CLASS USN YOU ARE INVITED TO
SEND HIM FREE VIA THIS BUREAU A TWENTY-FIVE WORD MESSAGE.
EVERY EFFORT TO EFFECT DELIVERY THIS MESSAGE BEFORE HIS
RETURN TO UNITEDSTATES WILL BE MADE FURTHER DETAILS
WILL BA FURNISHED YOU PROMOTPLY WHEN RECEIVED I REJOICE
WITH YOU IN THIS GOOD NEWS AND HOPE THAT HE WILL
COMMUNICATE WITH YOU AT A EARLY DATE=

    VICE ADMIRAL LOUIS DEFELD THE CHIEF OF NAVAL
PERSONNEL.

    854A

Official notice of Peter's liberation.

given X-rays. On the morning of September 13, I woke to someone shaking my bunk. It was Dr. Van Peenen. He had also arrived at the Oakland hospital and began asking about his OR crew from Guam. Someone told him where my bunk was. After asking how I was, he asked me if I still wanted to work with him. I thanked him for the offer, but told him I wanted to get into the laboratory field.

After our checkups in Oakland we were allowed to choose the naval hospital nearest our home town. I chose USNH Norman, Oklahoma. I boarded a C-27 that carried only about fifteen passengers. We stopped for fuel once in Arizona and arrived at the naval station in Olathe, Kansas at night to change planes.

All along the way people kept asking us questions. I was tired, sleepy and irritated at being questioned. I didn't know my serial number. I had last seen it on pay day just before the outbreak of the war. We didn't wear dog tags then. On one plane the pilot said something to the guy questioning me, who then apologized and said everything was okay. Our next and last plane ride was to Norman, Oklahoma.

We underwent more examinations at the USNH there. We were diagnosed as POW (no disease) and told we would be given ninety days rehabilitation leave. I filled out the leave request to start September 29 so I could be home at Christmas time. As soon as I arrived at Norman, I called Edith again and told here where I was. Two days later she and Mom called me from a motel room in downtown Norman and then they came to see me.

It was my first time seeing my mother since February 1940. I told her and Edith I would be arriving on a bus at the Phillipsburg station about 4:00 a.m. September 29. On September 27, I had already turned in my temporary liberty card when I got a call from my brother Felix. He had been home on leave, but had been ordered to report to San Diego. He was at the bus station in Norman with a four hour layover. I got my liberty card back and visited with him for a few hours. Later that night, just as I was about to go to sleep, about fifty more POWs were brought to the hospital. I knew several of them, but had not seen them since 1942. We talked all night long. I boarded the bus that next afternoon and finally fell asleep sometime after midnight. The next thing I knew I had arrived at Phillipsburg. Edith and my brother Billy were there to greet me. Billy hugged me. It was probably the first time he had ever hugged a man. I slept in my old bed upstairs that night.

September 22, 1945

Dearest Corrine and Harriet,

Yesterday was the most wonderful day of my life! With no exceptions. We walked in on Peter B at hospital here. He is not in bed—is only staying until his papers coming through. You know all records were lost, and they have so much to fix up. He looks <u>grand</u>! Is brown as a berry and hard as nails. His face and hands show the hardships he has been through. Face is tired looking and hand so calloused. But that is all in the past now. He has been checked and rechecked and is O.K...I am the happiest person that ever lived and can never get through thanking God for sparing my boys. Poor mothers who will never get their boys back!

Excerpt from a letter from Nora Marshall to her daughters Corrine and Harriet after meeting Peter B. in Norman, Oklahoma upon his return from Japan.

90-Days Leave

IT SEEMED LIKE I HAD JUST GOTTEN TO SLEEP WHEN MY family woke me up early the next morning. There was going to be a big welcome home party for me and Mom wanted us all to be ready. Folks began arriving about 10:00 that morning, over 100 of them that day. Tables of food were set up in the yard. I was miserable, but had to pretend I was having a good time. It was a big honor to have people welcome me home, but all I wanted right then was to visit with my mother, brothers and sisters. Billy and Stanley were home on leave and soon Donald would be too. Mack was still in Europe and Felix in San Diego. Six of us Marshall brothers served in the armed services during the war.

After I had been home for over a month it was just Mom and I. I had so been looking forward to this time, but then I couldn't stand it. I had been in a room with so many people for so many years that I couldn't stand all the peace and quiet. When Mom went to bed early, about 8:00 or 9:00, I did too, but I couldn't get to sleep. After tossing and turning for an hour or so, I would get up, get dressed and go out. I had the loan of Edith's 1937 Chevy while I was on leave. I'd drive to the Duck Inn, a small café on US 66 about a mile east of Conway. It stayed open until midnight. I usually saw someone I knew and we would drink coffee and talk.

I went to visit Harry Talbot, my old coach and teacher. He wanted me to stop by and talk to his school about my

POW experience, but I wasn't ready to do that yet. I knew I couldn't talk to any group of people just yet.

I decided to look up Sammy Lebovitz, the first friend I had made on Guam. I hadn't seen him since Zentsuji and didn't know what had happened to him. I caught a bus to his hometown of St. Louis, checked into a hotel and got out the telephone book. No Lebovitz listed. The next morning I hailed a cab and asked to be taken to the middle of the Jewish section of St. Louis. After knocking on several doors and getting nowhere, I was invited into one woman's house. She got on the phone and called friends, asking for their help in locating Sammy's mother for me. Within half an hour she had located her. Sammy's sister and her husband told me to sit tight; they would come and pick me up. Sammy was okay. He was on his way home by ship. Sammy's father had died shortly after the start of the war and his mother had remarried. The mother and daughter went all out fixing a fancy dinner. Then they took me to the bus station. A few weeks later I heard from Sammy, thanking me for caring enough to go to such trouble to find out what had happened to him.

Billy arranged for a couple of dates for me before I even got home, but they were very young girls and I felt very uncomfortable. I hadn't even touched a girl, much less kissed one in years. I made a movie date with a girl I met at the Duck Inn. She was about my age, had a slight limp, wasn't bad looking and had a nice personality. When I picked her up on the night of our date her folks broke their necks being nice to me. Her father wanted me to take his Buick—the latest model before they quit making cars during the war. My '37 Chevy did look bad, but not that bad! It felt like they were trying to get their daughter married off and I wasn't about to get married. I don't remember anything about my date except that I took her straight home after the movie. After that experience, I stayed away from the Duck Inn.

In early November Donald got some leave and was home for a few days. Mom, Donald and I drove to Kansas to visit Jerome and his wife Ruth, Ethel and her husband Floyd.

By the time Donald left I was beginning to unwind. I helped a neighbor cut his corn. I just wanted to do some hard farm work again. Edith had written asking me to spend some time with her family in Jefferson City. They were converting their restaurant into a hardware store, so I said I'd come help out.

Edith was a good friend of Minnie Elder, married to Dode Elder. Their niece Faye Elder, who had just turned eighteen, was working at the Missouri Public Expenditure Survey Office in Jefferson City. Edith and Minnie arranged for Faye, her younger sister Idabelle, Jessie Logue (Faye's stepmother's brother) and me to go to the Missouri-Oklahoma football game on Saturday in Columbia. This was the first time I had met any of them, so it was a blind date.

After the football game, the four of us took in a movie in Jefferson City. I made sure I was sitting next to Faye. Jessie said he needed to get back to Lebanon. I didn't know whether or not he had any romantic interest in Faye, but I wanted him away from her, so I told him that I was going back to the farm and would be glad to give him a lift.

I think I was home two nights and one day to get my clothes in order. Monday before returning to Jefferson City, I borrowed $600 from the State Bank in Lebanon. The owner of the bank knew all about me and gave me a signature loan. I told him I would repay it as soon as I received my back pay. I called Faye at work as soon as I got to Jefferson City. She suggested a place we could meet for lunch. We had lunch together and went out about every night for the next ten days or so. She wanted to stay with her dad and stepmother in Lebanon on Sunday evening. I drove her back to Jefferson City. Even though it was 10:30 or 11:00 by the time we got there, we went to one of our favorite parking places, where I proposed.

The next day, I went to a jewelry shop in Jefferson City and paid $110 for a diamond ring-wedding band set. I know that isn't much to spend, but I was kind of dumb about things like that.

On December 27 I boarded a bus back to USNH in Norman, Oklahoma. The doctors there didn't like my chest X-rays and kept me as a patient while ordering numerous tests over a three month period. They finally decided I was okay.

I Re-Enlist and
Get Married

I WAS ORDERED TO REPORT TO THE NAVAL TRAINING CENTER at Great Lakes, Illinois within ten days of my release. I caught a bus back to Phillipsburg. After being home a few days I bought a '38 Chevy for $600. It was much nicer looking than Edith's '37 had been. I then returned to Jefferson City for a few days. Faye and I decided we would wait to get married until I received my new orders from the naval training center at Great Lakes. Then I would come back to Lebanon, we'd get married and go together to my next duty station.

When I got to Great Lakes, they told me to report to the separation center. I said I was trying to reenlist, that my enlistment had expired in November 1945. It was now March, 1946. I was told I would receive ten weeks of retraining at the USNH independent duty school in Portsmouth, Virginia. This was recommended for all PHM second class and above who had been overseas for an extended period of time. I reenlisted for two more years, receiving a $300 bonus ($50 a year for each year I had served). I was promoted to PHM first class and given my orders to report to the independent duty school within one week. That was on a Thursday afternoon.

I called Faye and told her to put the wedding plans in motion. She called the Methodist Church in Lebanon, where she was a member, and reserved the church and the minister

Faye and Pete during engagement

for Sunday afternoon at 2:00. She also lined up a former high school classmate to play the organ, and submitted her resignation to her boss at work.

I drove all night, arriving at her Aunt Minnie's about 4:00 a.m. I crawled in bed with Faye and Idabelle with all my clothes on, kissed Faye and fell asleep. Missouri had a three day waiting period and a pre-marital blood test law. We went to the judge to get a waiver on the waiting period and then headed to the state laboratory for our blood tests.

Everything went off like clockwork. Idabelle was maid of honor; my brother Billy was best man. Faye had bought

Peter and Faye at wedding

a very pretty blue suit to be married in. Billy and I were in our uniforms. From my family there was Mack and his wife Ruby, Edith and George and Mom. From Faye's family were her dad Ralph and her stepmother Ethel, Minnie, Dode, her Grandmother Elder, her brother LeRoy and his wife Marie, and her brother Billy Ray. There were a few neighbors and friends also.

I'm sure everyone in the church could hear my knees knock as we walked down the aisle. There was a reception afterwards at her Grandmother Elder's home. Faye's Aunt Minnie baked their cake. I think George, Ralph and Dode had spiked the punch. There seemed to be an awful lot of laughing. When we got ready to leave, Billy told us to get in the car and he would load our suitcases. He did that, but he also wired about a dozen tin cans to the rear bumper.

When I checked in at the naval training station, they directed us to where there was naval housing for married sailors and wives in Alexandria Park. It was nothing fancy, but looked like a mansion to us. It was $30 a month which I think equaled the extra I received for living in off base housing.

The ten week training course was a happy period. I felt like I was back in the navy. I studied hard and made better than average grades. Faye was a good cook. We went sightseeing every weekend. During the training course a list of naval training schools was posted on the bulletin board. I requested the clinical laboratory techniques at the USN medical center in Bethesda, Maryland. It was a twenty-four week course.

About the middle of my training at Portsmouth I was asked to report to the record office. The chief in charge said he had noticed that I was a POW and that upon the recommendation of the CO I could be promoted four positions. He said I was acting chief that day and permanent appointment chief the next day. The extra money was a big plus.

My request for laboratory school was approved and sometime in June we headed for Bethesda.

Bethesda

W E COULDN'T FIND A PLACE TO RENT IN BETHESDA SO, AFTER staying in hotel rooms for a few days, Faye went back to Portsmouth and moved in with Alice, another navy wife, in the same Alexandria Park. Her husband, Doc, was in property and accounting school. We split the rent for our wives' housing. Doc and I stayed on the base at Bethesda Sunday night through Friday night. All the schools had tests on Saturday morning, and we would be restricted to base if we didn't pass with a seventy percent or higher. I never really had any problems with the tests. Doc and I always had all our things packed and in the car ready to leave when the tests were done about 11:30 a.m. It was a four to five hour drive from Bethesda to Portsmouth. We stayed until about 10:00 p.m. Sunday nights. One Saturday Doc didn't come back to Portsmouth with me; Faye wanted to ride part way with me and then catch a bus back to Portsmouth. She ended up riding all the way to D.C. where I took her to the bus station for her return trip.

I finally found a basement room in Bethesda for $60 a month. The bathroom only had a toilet and a wash basin. We used the laundry tub for sponge baths. We cooked our meals on a double burner hot plate. We managed okay.

Faye always helped me with my studying at night. That's how she knew about the Rh factor when she learned she was pregnant. After her first obstetric exam she was referred to

Walter Reed Hospital. She asked, "Am I Rh negative?" They were surprised that she knew about Rh factor.

I completed the training with an overall grade average of ninety percent and was assigned to the Marine Corps air station in Cherry Point, North Carolina in December 1946. I was put in charge of the laboratory, which included four enlisted employees besides me. This was not a naval hospital, but was a very large dispensary. The lab officer was a three-month rotating position among four doctors.

We spent the first month in a Quonset hut, and then were given permanent housing on base. It was by far the nicest place we had lived in. Faye was having no problems in her pregnancy. Fresh from lab school, I was rapidly updating all our lab procedures and reagents. I had worked very hard getting everything squared away at work and home.

I was contacted by an official from the War Department, following through on a report I had given naval intelligence on Guam. I dictated to him about Japanese mistreatment of American POWs. After signing the typed up statement, I thought that was the end of dealing with the war.

I began feeling run down in January 1947, but I just ignored it and kept going. By mid-February I was having cold sweats, a low grade fever and coughing spells. I had no energy. Finally I went to the sick bay where the doctor made a rapid diagnosis of tuberculosis.

He said it was a tentative diagnosis and would have to be confirmed at the USNH in Camp Lejeune, North Carolina, but he told me there was no doubt that it was TB. I begged the doctor to allow me to stay until after the baby was born sometime in early March. The doctors were cooperative and I wrote asking Mom if she would come out if I paid all her expenses. In hindsight, I shouldn't have done that as Faye had everything under control, but you don't think straight from a hospital bed.

Shortly after midnight on March 5, Faye called the dispensary to come and get her. She woke me up to tell me the baby was coming soon. Cynthia Lynn Marshall was born a few hours later and I was sent to Camp Lejeune the same day.

Camp Lejeune

THE DIAGNOSIS OF TB WAS CONFIRMED. MOM ARRIVED AT Cherry Point. Faye and Cynthia went home from the dispensary. Faye received a phone call from a representative of the Red Cross, checking up on Faye's welfare. She told Faye that Edith (my sister) had told her that Faye was a hysterical, pregnant young female that didn't know how to cope when I came down with TB. Edith had demanded that the Red Cross send her daily reports on our condition. Edith had said she was very busy with her business and couldn't take the time off to do so herself.

Faye was furious and rightfully so. Everything was under control. When I had asked Mom to come out, I didn't realize that I had just given her another responsibility. Faye told the Red Cross worker that she would report her to the navy department if she heard of any more poking into her life. She also forbid her to give Edith any information, told her a few truths about Edith, and made it very clear that we had not asked for any help. That ended that!

Faye drove down to see me twice before I was sent to the USNH in St. Albans, New York. Faye had the navy ship our belongings back to Walnut Glen farm. She sold our car. Then she, Mom and Cynthia flew back to Missouri. It wasn't practical for her and the baby to live on the farm. Her grandmother Elder was the closest thing to a mother Faye had, and she lived in nearby Lebanon. Faye and Cynthia moved in with her.

USNH, St. Albans

THE HOSPITAL HAD ONLY TWO TYPES OF PATIENTS: TB patients and WWII vets who needed reconstructive surgery. I arrived in April 1947.

At this point, bed rest was the main treatment; however, various forms of surgery were being tried on some patients. Crushing the phrenic nerve caused the diaphragm to lift up. This helped when a cavity was in the lower portion of the lung. The surgeons also had some success with inserting small plastic balls to temporarily collapse a certain portion of the lung, allowing that area to heal. Thoracoplasty was effective, but it was permanent. In this procedure, certain ribs are removed to cause a collapse of the lungs in the area of the cavity. This drastic measure was used for patients with far advanced TB. An introduced pneumothorax (air or gas in pleural space of the chest cavity) was used quite often.

After all the X-rays and examinations, my diagnosis was complete—tuberculosis, moderately advanced. My left lung was heavily infiltrated. There were two spots on my right lung that worried the doctors. The ward doctor had a long talk with me. He said my naval career was over; however, since I was a POW I could not be discharged until my TB was in an arrested state. I could be sent to a VA hospital only upon my request. Since I was drawing about $60 a month more as a chief than I would be with 100 percent disability in a VA hospital, I chose to be treated in the navy. The doctor said that they would begin pneumothorax on me starting the following Monday. Once a week, air would be injected into the pleural cavity to keep a portion of my lung collapsed.

I didn't care for that form of treatment, but I wasn't the doctor. Monday came and went with no pneumothorax. Tuesday the doctor had another talk with me. He was a sensitive individual and realized my displeasure with the pneumothorax. Against his better judgment, he was going to try bed rest only for the next three months and then reevaluate my condition. It was a good decision. X-rays showed improvement.

For the next one-and-a-half years I lived a daily routine. I was in a glass cubicle with six other beds. There were two doors opening to the cubicle from the hallway. At one end of the cubicle was a bathroom, which I was allowed to walk to and from. When we got clean linen I made my own bed. We were allowed a radio if it had earphones so as not to disturb the other patients. Vital signs were taken at 6:00 a.m., breakfast at 7:00, and lunch at noon. Quiet hours—no reading, no radio or anything—from 1:00 to 3:00 p.m. We either slept or pretended to sleep. Dinner was between 5:00 and 6:00. We got a snack—a sandwich and milk or chocolate milk—at 8:00 p.m. Once a month before breakfast, a rubber tube was introduced into my stomach and fluid suctioned off and cultured for TB. I had one positive in May 1947; all the other smears and cultures were negative.

Faye was getting a dependent's allowance; all the rest of my money was going into the bank. My total monthly expenses were about $5.00. I took three New York newspapers. The Morning Mirror and Daily News were two cents apiece; the evening paper was five cents. I read every word, including the ads. I wrote Faye four or five letters a week. I read every book on bridge I could get my hands on.

One day in 1947 I was ordered to get dressed. I was then taken in a wheel chair to the captain's office where I received a letter of commendation for my work during the battle of Guam. The captain said that Captain Lineberry had recommended this before he died. I assume that Dr. Van Peenen also had something to do with it.

Faye came out on the train to see me Christmas 1947 and they allowed me to see Cynthia in the doctor's office. During their visit there was a terrible snow storm, the worst in eighty years, and Faye was unable to make it to the hospital a couple of days.

Sometime in 1947 or 1948 I was subpoenaed to testify at the war trial in Japan, but because of my TB I was not allowed to attend.

I had followed every rule, regulation, and all the other junk thrown in, but by June 1948 I was about to blow a gasket! I got permission to see my doctor in his office and asked if I could get a ten day leave. He said I hadn't had a positive culture since my first month at St. Albans in May 1947. My left lung was clearing up nicely, but he was still worried about the two spots on my right lung. He gave me my leave.

I called the bank to wire me some money. I called TWA and they indicated they could probably get me on a plane to St. Louis the next morning. My flight had a tail wind and it took only three and a half hours to arrive in St. Louis. From there I caught a bus to Lebanon—a four hour ride.

It sure felt good to be out of the hospital for a few days. The Lebanon Daily News sent a photographer to Grandma Elder's, where Faye and Cynthia were staying, for a picture of me.

Back in St. Albans after my return I was allowed to walk to and from the mess hall three times a day for meals to start

Peter, Faye and Cynthia in Lebanon

building my strength back up. By August I still had to observe quiet hours each afternoon, but otherwise I could stay up as long as I wanted.

They were getting ready to discharge me as an arrested case of TB. I requested to be sent to the VA Hospital at Springfield, Missouri. I wanted my records to be in a VA hospital. The navy gave me a series of tests to help guide me in seeking a future career. According to their results, I would be an ideal social worker. However, when I expressed an interest in going to college and getting my degree in medical technology, they said there was nothing in my test results that would keep me from being a good medical technologist.

In the middle of July 1948 I received my honorable discharge from the navy. It was a discharge for medical reasons, but, unless you were someone working in a naval records hospital, you wouldn't know the difference from any honorable discharge.

Springfield VA hospital is about forty miles from Walnut Glen farm. I was worked up—medical history, X-rays, etc. The doctor who did this stopped and stared at me. He said, "You shouldn't still be alive."

After observing me for about six weeks, I was released. They came to the same conclusions as had the navy. As the navy doctors had done, they cautioned me to really take it easy for four to five years. It would be okay to go to school, but not to do any hard physical work.

Lebanon

WHEN I GOT OUT OF THE HOSPITAL WE STAYED WITH FAYE'S grandmother in Lebanon. I went to the VA and explained to them that I wanted to go to college majoring in medical technology. Disabled veterans were eligible to go to school under Public Law 16. It had some advantages over the other GI schooling, but first your major had to be approved by the VA. I was sent to the VA in Kansas City for some tests, including one which was given to freshmen at Ohio State University. I scored in the 92nd percentile. The VA counselor thought I was aiming too low, but I told him I knew myself. I got approval to attend college under PL 16 and major in medical technology.

Arizona State University was on the VA list of approved schools offering the major I wanted. Both Faye and I wanted to get away from Missouri. ASU accepted my high school grades and I was given a letter of admission for the semester beginning in February 1949.

Faye learned she was pregnant again and began the usual prenatal workup. We didn't know when we would be back in Missouri again, so we visited family along the way to Phoenix, Arizona—our destination.

Phoenix

WE ARRIVED IN PHOENIX ON THANKSGIVING DAY 1948. WE rented a very small place in a trailer court in east Phoenix. There were community showers and my good watch was stolen while I showered. With our income of $138 a month VA disability it was impossible to find a place to rent. So we cashed in our two $1,000 government bonds and a life insurance policy to make a large down payment on a house in West Phoenix. Our monthly payments were about $60.

We quickly learned about the hidden costs in getting settled in our new home. By the time we got everything squared away, our bank account was depleted. My VA check was late due to many changes of address in a short period of time. I walked to the nearest grocer, a Chinese market two blocks away, and asked if I could run a grocery bill until I received my VA check. I must have an honest face because he agreed. This began a long association with the Sun Valley Market.

It was a madhouse during registration week in February 1949, but I eventually got squared away on my PL 16, got the courses I wanted and was given a bookstore card that allowed me free books. By going to summer school I was able to get my degree in just over three years. My monthly income was $258.00.

I was studying for a test when our second daughter, Beverly Lea Marshall, was born on April 29, 1949. I had to borrow $75 until my check came in before I could pay the hospital bill at St. Joseph's.

$1368 Compensation Check

S OMETIME IN 1950 I SAW AN ARTICLE IN THE ARIZONA REPUB-
lic newspaper that stated all American POWs were to be
compensated $1.00 for every day we weren't fed according to
the international law for prisoners of war. The money came
from frozen German and Japanese assets in the United States.
The American Red Cross was one of the agencies listed as
having the proper forms to fill out to get our money. I was
the first person in their office when it opened the day after
the article. Within a few weeks I had my $1368 –the largest
received by anyone living in Phoenix. We paid our bills then
bought some clothes, which we desperately needed.

Seniors majoring in medical technology had to spend a
full twelve months training on the job at one of three hos-
pitals in Phoenix, after receiving approval from the hospital.
I applied at Memorial Hospital where Dr. Rosenthal interviewed me. When he learned that I had actually performed
clinical lab work in the navy, he wanted me for night call in
their lab. It had been four years since I had last worked and
needed some intensive retraining for a few days.

The on-call job at Memorial's lab became mine three days
later. The extra $175 a month was sorely needed. Since I lived
only ten minutes away, I stayed home while on call, between
5:00 p.m. and 7:00 a.m. every night. This was early 1951 and
I had this job for two and one half years. During my senior
year I was going to school at Memorial Hospital during the

Peter and Cynthia when $1368 check arrived

day. There were only three of us students.

Dr. Rosenthal gave a few lectures, but mostly the technicians were in charge of our training and gave us our written tests. Training also included watching an autopsy from beginning to end.

The worst job I had was drawing blood from polio patients in iron lungs. To collect the specimens you had to stick your arms through the port holes. You knew you were hurting the patients by straightening out their arms enough to draw the blood. It wore me out absolutely.

I passed my finals and received my diploma in May 1952. I now had my Bachelor of Science in Medical Technology. However, I still had to finish my full twelve months of training

Cynthia, Beverly and Faye, 1950

which ended in late June. I then worked full time at Memorial Hospital and also kept my on-call job at night. The $258 I had received monthly while going to school had dropped to a percentage of VA disability. Mine was thirty percent.

In the spring of 1953 Congress passed a bill awarding POWs $1.50 per day that they were mistreated while a prisoner of war. My check came to $2,042. Again the funds were taken from frozen German and Japanese assets from WWII. I felt real good about taking this money. We were hurting financially when we received the check.

The TB Returns

ONE MORNING WHEN I WENT TO WORK, DR. CLAYPOOL, THE flight surgeon for the Arizona National Guard was waiting for me. The guard had a new building and was expanding and a position had opened up. It was full time and paid $351 a month. I would have to join the Air Force Reserve with staff sergeant ranking. I would also be paid for that rank for the one weekend duty each month plus two weeks maneuvers yearly. I would also get two weeks of vacation a year. However, I would have to waive my VA disability payments.

When I told Dr. Claypool about my TB history, he said he would go ahead and sign me up and then see what happened. I gave my two week notice to Memorial Hospital. I had already quit my night job because it had begun to affect me. I jumped every time the phone rang at night.

My duties were primarily to screen new recruits and give them as much of a physical exam as I could. I told those I thought would pass to come back on the weekend each month when Dr. Claypool would be there. I kept their records and made sure all were blood typed and shots were up to date.

About the third week there, Dr. Claypool made an appointment for me to see Dr. Netzer, Chief of Service at the VA hospital in Tucson. Dr. Netzer found nothing on the physical, but ordered an X-ray. He also sent to the VA for all X-rays I'd had since arriving in Phoenix. At the time, I went for a TB checkup each February. I had been told that my TB was stable.

About six weeks after I started this job, I received a telephone call at night from Dr. Claypool. "I have some bad news for you, Pete." Beginning in February 1953 there was evidence of active TB in my right upper lobe. The two most recent X-rays showed honeycomb formations in the right upper lobe with the possibility of cavities. Dr. Netzer recommended that I be hospitalized immediately and chemotherapy treatments be initiated. They were sending a copy of the report to the Phoenix VA office.

I was devastated. I shouldn't have bought the new car. I shouldn't have changed jobs, waiving my VA disability pay. We shouldn't have taken the vacation back to Missouri over the summer, spending a lot of money. We had no money coming in and I didn't know how long it would be before the VA disability pay would begin again. We had house payments, car payments and furniture payments to make. But we only felt sorry for ourselves for about one day. We had a lot to do in a short time.

I didn't wait for the VA to notify me officially. I called them the next day saying I would be reporting into the VA hospital in Tucson, but needed a week to get my affairs in order. Fortunately, I had a good credit rating, always making payments on time. I told my sad story to the bank where I owed car and furniture payments. They were most cooperative. The car was refinanced for two years with first payment in forty five days. For the furniture, I was told if I could make one quarter of the monthly payment, or as a last resort pay the interest each month, they wouldn't pressure me.

Faye went to the unemployment bureau to take tests in applying for a job. We had always wanted both children to be in school before she went to work, but we had no choice now. We decided if I could borrow $200 it would be enough to keep our heads above water. I called a classmate who had also majored in medical technology with me and who was a survivor of the Bataan Death March. He loaned me the money without hesitation.

VA Hospital Tucson

W HEN I BOARDED THE BUS TO TUCSON IN LATE JULY 1953, Faye and I had done what we could to keep the Marshall household in order. After her typing tests and interview, Faye was told she would have no trouble getting a job, which she did at Memorial Hospital in the business office. She hired a housekeeper/babysitter for our girls. Cynthia was in school in first grade most of the day. It was really tough, but Faye managed.

I received many X-rays from all angles. My left lung still looked stable. But those two spots that had worried the doctors in 1947 and 1948 were now cavities. There was honeycomb formation in the upper part of the upper lobe of my right lung. This meant that the entire area could form a large cavity with hemorrhaging. In 1947-48 streptomycin had been the only antibiotic used to treat TB, and then only in those cases with TB meningitis. The only available streptomycin had many impurities and often destroyed the nerve controlling balance. By 1953 it was more purified and antibiotics INH and PAS were now available.

The doctors were also doing segmental resections on some patients now and I was considered a good prospect for surgery. At this time they also didn't know the most effective combinations of drugs to use as they were all relatively new, and they were trying to figure it out. As a result, Patient A received streptomycin and INH, Patient B got streptomycin and PAS, Patient C, INH and PAS, and Patient D got all three. I was put on streptomycin (intramuscular twice a week) and PAS (liquid form daily). PAS tasted so terrible that I had to bite on a lemon before taking it. It went right through me, staining my pajamas front and back. After a few weeks I began reacting to PAS and was put on streptomycin and INH, which I would stay on for several years. My ward doctor told me that as soon as the antibiotics had "cooled off" my active TB, I would be sent to the surgeon, Dr. Carr.

I applied for 100 percent disability back to February 1953, when all the doctors had said the change in the X-ray was visible. I even wrote Arizona Senator Barry Goldwater and Congressman John Rhodes asking them to help me with my claim. However, without a positive smear or culture in February, I had no legitimate claim. The X-rays were not enough. I hoped that the doctor who examined me back then received some kind of punishment.

Although Faye was working and had plenty to do on weekends, she drove to Tucson with Cynthia and Beverly every third weekend. She and the girls came on a Saturday morning and stayed overnight with Edith and George, who were living in Tucson. This was very difficult for Faye after what Edith had done to her when Cynthia was born.

I responded very well to streptomycin and INH. During the last week of December 1953, Dr. Carr, the chest surgeon, had a long talk with me. He could save a portion of my right upper lobe. While inside my chest, he wanted to do a decortication of my right lower lobe. That pleural infusion done by the doctor in the POW camp in 1944 had left all kinds of adhesions in my lower lobe. Dr. Carr wanted to free the area to give me full use of that lobe. He explained that even after he cut out the area with the cavities and honeycomb formation, I would still have to remain on antibiotics for years. First, he wanted me on the surgery ward for a few weeks of pre-surgery diet.

There were two to a room on the surgery ward. We had a steak every night for dinner. My roommate was in such bad condition, he could only eat a few bites of his steak, so I finished it off for him. He said it did his heart good to see a man eat like I did! I was scheduled for surgery in February 1954.

Surgery

FAYE TOOK A FEW DAYS OFF WORK TO BE WITH ME DURING surgery. On the night before, I was strapped to an adjustable table with my head tilted sharply downward for thirty minutes in order to drain off any fluid in the lung area. I was shaved on my right side from head to waist. I was on penicillin and another drug to cut down the possibility of infection. I was given a huge, painful shot of vitamin K. On the morning of surgery, I was given something to calm me down. Faye said I acted drunk.

When they wheeled me into surgery I looked at the clock: just past 7:30 a.m. I made sure they had the right blood (A positive). The anesthesiologist put the needle in my vein and told me to start counting backwards from 99. I got as far as 92 when my lights went out. When I came to, they were just finishing sewing me up. I saw the clock, but couldn't focus. When I asked, they told me it was 1:30 p.m. I felt no pain. Faye said she heard me asking for my wife as they wheeled me to my room. Dr. Carr had already talked to her about an hour earlier, telling her that everything went just as he had planned. He didn't stick around for the insertion of drainage tubes and closing.

That evening was a nightmare. Every time they gave me a shot for pain I got sick, so they finally switched to morphine. The next day I was doing okay and Faye decided it was wise for her to go home. On the third night I woke up feeling a bubbling under my collar bone and around my eyes. I pressed the button for the nurse who then called Dr. Carr. He showed up within ten minutes.

After surgery my drainage tubes were hooked up to a vacuum pump. When you have lung surgery, for a few days you lose a little air through the incision area every time you breathe. That was the reason for the vacuum pump. A blood clot had stopped up one of my drainage tubes. Dr. Carr took care of it, assuring me that I was okay. I wasn't hurting, just worried. From that day on, I had no more problems with my TB. Five days after surgery, my stitches and tubes were removed, and physical therapy began. Physical therapy continued through the rest of my hospital stay. Dr. Carr wanted me on his ward for six weeks following surgery.

After about four weeks, I felt I just had to get out of there for a few days; the walls were closing in on me. I asked Dr. Carr for a two day pass. He calmed me down, saying I had done so well that it would be foolish to take a chance now. If I would stick around for four more weeks with no complications, he would release me for good. I agreed. In a couple of weeks I was transferred to the "country club" ward for patients soon on their way out of the hospital.

Going Home to my Family

EIGHT WEEKS AFTER SURGERY I WENT TO SEE DR. NOON, THE ward doctor, and asked to leave the hospital. He said I wasn't ready. Then I asked to go home for a few days and he repeated that I wasn't ready. Then I made a mistake and said that Dr. Carr had said I could. Dr. Noon informed me that he was my doctor now; that Dr. Carr was himself in a VA hospital in Texas having chest surgery due to complications from Valley Fever.

After lying awake most of the night thinking, I decided I would leave. As soon as Dr. Noon arrived the next morning I informed him of my decision. I also asked him to write a memo to the VA hospital in Phoenix indicating what medication I was on. He not only refused but blew his stack, saying that anyone as dumb as I deserved to die!

I got a check-out list and went through all the proper procedures checking out with the post office, Red Cross, record office, etc. I couldn't button the jeans I had arrived in some nine months ago, having gained about twenty pounds. I managed to buckle my belt in the first hole and wore my shirt on the outside. I called George to come and take me to the bus station and asked to borrow $10 to buy my ticket. That was the first and last time I borrowed money from a relative. As I was leaving the ward to go outside to wait for George, Dr. Noon's secretary gave me a memo listing the medication I was taking. She also told me what doctor to give it to at the VA hospital in Phoenix.

I got to the bus station in Phoenix and called Faye at work to come get me. I know she must have been awfully worried, not only about my health, but about the possibility of me losing my VA disability. But I just knew that everything would be okay.

We let the babysitter go. On Monday I went to the VA and received a month's supply of INH pills. They told me to come in each Tuesday and Friday for my streptomycin shots. They also wrote a letter to the VA hospital in Tucson asking for my records and recommendation for my disposition. In a couple of weeks, Dr. Steiner, the Chief of TB service in Tucson, answered the letter. He said that in his opinion I was ready to be released from the hospital and that I should not be disciplined for going against medical advice when I left. After about the tenth trip to the hospital for my shot, I told the doctor that my wife was a nurse and asked if they could give me a syringe, needles and streptomycin to take home so she could give me my shots. They agreed and gave me three month's supply of INH and streptomycin. Afterwards, I came in every three months for checkup and to pick up my medical supplies.

After taking the streptomycin shots for about three months, I began to get the strangest sensation within about an hour of getting the shot. While it didn't hurt, it felt like worms were crawling under my skin. The doctor was not concerned. The symptoms went away within a day.

One day when I went in for my three month checkup, there was Dr. Noon from Tucson. He had been transferred to the Phoenix VA. He didn't recognize me, perhaps because he had never seen me in anything but hospital pajamas. We got along fine.

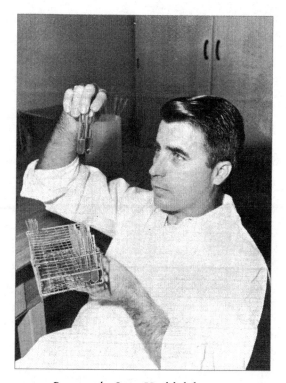

Peter at the State Health laboratory

It was now October 1954. I had become a full time house husband—ironing, sewing, cleaning house, cooking. Once I had the iron too hot and evaporated some fancy lace on one of the kids' dresses. I hated ironing Faye's circular skirts; it took forever. However, I guess I was doing okay because Faye didn't complain.

Sometime in November I got permission to return to work and I flooded the area with applications. I got an interview with Dr. Crecelius at the Arizona State Health Laboratory. He told me to go to the merit system and get on the available list. I had to pass a written test above a certain score. I would receive five points extra for being a veteran and another five points for being a disabled veteran. I passed and got a job in the serology department at the state lab, beginning a twenty-six year career there, ending in my retirement in February 1981 as head of serology. I owe much to Dr. Crecelius, one of the finest people I have known. Just as Harry Talbot and Dr. Van Peenen had done, he brought out the best in me.

Epilogue

MY TB NEVER RETURNED, BUT I EXPERIENCED POST-TRAU-matic stress periodically, usually at times of observance of significant events of WWII, such as the anniversary of Pearl Harbor. I don't know what I would have done without Faye at such times.

Congress passed a couple of bills that helped me out financially after my retirement. One acknowledged that I would have gone up in rank during the period of captivity and awarded me back pay for the difference. Another was a one-time payout to POWs and my share was about $20,000.

In 1993 I wrote a memoir of my life growing up on Walnut Glen, my POW experiences, and my work. Faye typed every page and we made copies for our children and grandchildren. A good portion of what I wrote has been included in this book.

A few years later, I wrote a more detailed account of the 1368 days I spent as a prisoner of war. I sent a copy to the Lebanon newspapter, which published an article about me. Roger Mansell, a historian writing a book about POWs captured on Guam (*Captured, The Forgotten Men of Guam*), saw the article on the Internet and contacted me, asking for an interview. I agreed and we had two telephone interviews lasting about an hour each. He sent me the typed copy of each session and I reviewed it for accuracy.

After I broke down several times during each of these interviews, Roger asked me what percent VA disability I received. I told him I had thirty percent, the minimum amount for a vet who had had lung surgery. He told me I should be getting 100 percent and that he could put me in touch with people who could help me with the application process. He had done this for many ex-POWs over the course of his research for his book. I talked it over with the family, who all urged me to go for it, especially since it could mean survivor benefits for Faye when I died.

Roger gave me the name of a marine captain who had served on Guam, who had gotten his PhD after the war and devoted his life to helping veterans. This person gave me the phone number of a contact in Sun City, who volunteered each Wednesday helping the vets. I called and made an appointment to see him. He handled all the paperwork for the application and scheduled all the necessary doctor appointments—medical, eye, hearing, and psychiatrist. I also had to be seen by a social worker. The appointments were spread out over many months.

The medical exam found a herniated disk and gave me ten percent additional credit for that. The eye exam gave me no additional credit, nor did I expect any. The hearing exam found that I was deaf in one ear and had only a small percentage of hearing in the other ear, but did not give me any additional credit. This was discouraging because there is a distinct correlation between the drugs used to treat my TB and a subsequent loss of hearing.

The social worker was a Vietnam War veteran. He channeled his anger at that war and the poor treatment he received upon his return into helping other vets. Faye attended these sessions with me at his recommendation. They were painful and all three of us were in tears. He acknowledged my PTSD and recommended I should receive 100 percent disability.

The last exam was with the psychiatrist. She agreed with

Peter and Faye on her 80th Birthday

the social worker and two months later I received official notice of a determination of 100 percent disability, retroactive to my application some eighteen months earlier. This finding solved my financial worries, even allowing me to put aside savings each month.

Faye died in 2013. We were married sixty-seven years. She was the glue that held the family together through all the years I spent battling TB. She was the love of my life from the moment we met and I miss her every day. We raised two daughters, Cynthia and Beverly, who now take very good care of their father. We have two grandchildren and six great grandchildren.

Faye is buried in the National Memorial Cemetery in Cave Creek, Arizona. When my time comes, I will be buried with her. It is a peaceful place. We will be resting in good company among my fellow veterans.

51612593R00084

Made in the USA
San Bernardino, CA
27 July 2017